Performing Political Theory

"This splendid volume introduces students to the works of some of the most influential modern political philosophers, highlighting the various rhetorical or 'performative' strategies they employed. It is a timely and welcome work that will be of great help to undergraduate and graduate students alike."
—Professor Timothy Burns, *Baylor University, U.S.A., Editor of Interpretation*

"This highly readable and accessible new book offers an intriguing take on political theory. Showing that classic texts can be like 'scripts' that are 'performed', Uhr explores new ideas of dialogue between text and reader, prompting a refreshing approach to active engagement with theory in the classroom."
—Professor Michael Saward, *Warwick University, U.K.*

"*Performing Political Theory* shows that close attention to the rhetorical ambitions or 'performance' of major works of political philosophy is essential for understanding the substance of their teachings. It is a welcome and timely invitation to both students and teachers to enter the challenging, exhilarating and potentially liberating world of political thought."
—Professor Haig Patapan, *School of Government and International Relations, Griffith University, Australia*

John Uhr

Performing Political Theory

Pedagogy in Modern Political Theory

John Uhr
School of Politics and International
  Relations
Australian National University
Canberra, Australia

ISBN 978-981-10-7997-9   ISBN 978-981-10-7998-6 (eBook)
https://doi.org/10.1007/978-981-10-7998-6

Library of Congress Control Number: 2017964574

© The Editor(s) (if applicable) and The Author(s) 2018, corrected publication 2018
This work is subject to copyright. All rights are solely and exclusively licensed by the Publisher, whether the whole or part of the material is concerned, specifically the rights of translation, reprinting, reuse of illustrations, recitation, broadcasting, reproduction on microfilms or in any other physical way, and transmission or information storage and retrieval, electronic adaptation, computer software, or by similar or dissimilar methodology now known or hereafter developed.
The use of general descriptive names, registered names, trademarks, service marks, etc. in this publication does not imply, even in the absence of a specific statement, that such names are exempt from the relevant protective laws and regulations and therefore free for general use.
The publisher, the authors and the editors are safe to assume that the advice and information in this book are believed to be true and accurate at the date of publication. Neither the publisher nor the authors or the editors give a warranty, express or implied, with respect to the material contained herein or for any errors or omissions that may have been made. The publisher remains neutral with regard to jurisdictional claims in published maps and institutional affiliations.

Cover illustration: © Stephen Bonk/Fotolia.co.uk

Printed on acid-free paper

This Palgrave Pivot imprint is published by the registered company Springer Nature Singapore Pte Ltd. part of Springer Nature
The registered company address is: 152 Beach Road, #21-01/04 Gateway East, Singapore 189721, Singapore

Preface

This book began as the work of two Australian university colleagues who thought they could write up an account of their attempts to teach courses on the history of modern political theory: from Machiavelli through Nietzsche, with a brief look at a number of contemporary theorists. The first surprise was that there appeared to be very few books reviewing teaching practices in the general field of political theory. This was especially surprising given the heated professional debates which have surrounded conflicting interpretations of many core historical texts in modern political theory. There are very many books examining the contested nature of modern political theory, but the experts on the substance of political theory seem reluctant to examine the process of academic teaching of political theory.

With my teaching colleague at the Australian National University, Dr. William Bosworth, we approached Palgrave who generously provided us with a contract to prepare the planned book. We were confident that scholars interested in political theory might also be interested in our reflections on ways we have tried to teach this subject to undergraduate students over several years. Our aim has been to 'teach the texts' while leaving most of the knowledge of the surrounding 'contexts' to the excellent reports available from editors of anthologies such as *The Broadview Anthology of Social and Political Thought: Essential Readings* we relied on (Bailey et al. 2012). In our teaching, we relied on English-language editions of modern Western political thought. So too, in this book, my reports of pedagogy relate to English-speaking students learning to read English-language versions of political theories often originally published in another language: Italian, French and German being the main examples.

Some students seemed fascinated by those works (translated where necessary) by Machiavelli, Hobbes, Locke, Rousseau or Kant (and so on) to which we devoted our lectures and invited them to compare; many other students found it all a bit too dry and formal, as though 'theory' could be reduced to recollection of 'the text' or rather to more than a dozen competing 'texts'; and yet another group feared that we were befriending the enemy in our apparently misguided attempt to help students know more about the imposers and imposters who had done their best to hoodwink generations of readers into thinking that 'theory' basically meant submitting to the technical rationality of 'possessive individualism'—to apply the category of liberalism devised by Canadian political theorist C. B. Macpherson so many years ago.

As academic teachers, Dr. Boswell and I left it open to students to find their own ways of making sense of our recovery of what we thought were the main theories being presented by our gallery of intellectual giants. We assumed that contemporary students of politics and history would want to know what these influential giants thought was the nature of 'political theory'. For some students, that knowledge was important because this gallery included some of the most inspiring minds of the modern West; for others, it was important because each of us has to unearth our own independence by unravelling ourselves from the 'identities' and 'cultures' imposed on us as trusting followers of some rather distrustful theorists. The larger point was that conservative and progressive students still at least had to try to understand the type of political theory being worked through by each of these past masters, so that they better understood what was that they were either conserving or progressing—or even dismembering, as appeared to be the case for a number of radicals.

Our teaching tried to let students test their own pet theories of politics against the imposing power of the leading figures in modern political thought. The first and in many ways most fundamental challenge was helping students learn how to read classic texts: the great books of reflection in the history of the modern West. To our pleasant surprise, the American Political Science Association (APSA) came to our rescue. One of the Association's state of the art textbooks is Ada Finifter's edited collection *The State of the Discipline*, published in 1993. Included in this edited collection is a chapter we came to rely on: Arlene Saxonhouse's 'Texts and Canons: The Status of Great Books in Political Theory' (Saxonhouse 1993, 3–26). Saxonhouse had earlier published a provisional version 'Of Paradigms and Cores' in *Polity* in 1988 (Saxonhouse 1988, 409–418). The 1993 chapter became our highly valued commentary on the competing schools of interpretation around reading classic texts in political theory. One of Saxonhouse's special gifts is her ability to let students see how much turns on choices we make over instruments of interpretation. Of compelling interest is her articulation of gender as an important factor in how we today read texts written in earlier times. Also of great interest is her calm moderation of two of the rival schools of textual interpretation whose representatives often talk (loudly) past one another: the 'contextualist' contribution of Quentin Skinner and followers who value texts according to their place in 'historical context', compared to the curiously described 'instrumental' approach of Leo Strauss and followers, who value texts according to their contemporary educational value.

Saxonhouse has a more recent chapter on interpretation in political theory in the *Oxford Handbook of Political Theory* (Saxonhouse 2008, 844–858). She argues that political theorists have 'put aside too readily the practice of reading the great texts with sufficient care', preferring instead to study them 'as the expression of the historical context in which they were written'. She further notes that Strauss' complaints about the neglect of traditional interpretations of close textual reading were treated by the political science discipline as 'a shrill and readily dismissed response' to the growing marginalisation of political theory. Yet the leaders in textual theorising refused to accept the threatened marginal status. Saxonhouse cites three US-based European refugees as dominating the scholarship of textual interpretation: Hannah Arendt, Judith Shklar and Leo Strauss who in their 'profoundly different ways' pursued their 'constructive engagement with the texts of political theory'. Their aim was not the conventional one of wanting 'to know what was said, written, thought in the past'—as though we teach students in order to let them know the competing 'perspectives' on offer in the history of political thought. On the contrary, their aim was 'to learn from these works as teachers of questions, perspectives, truths that we tend to forget' under the pressure of everyday management of our immediate political activities (Saxonhouse 2008, 849–850, 854–855).

As academic teachers, we were impressed that political theory could be given such high prominence. A comprehensive textbook like the *Broadview Anthology* helps academic teachers present their accounts of modern political theory in ways which allow students to begin their serious engagement with the *theorising* and not simply the *words* locked into the core texts in modern political theory. But not every venture to clarify political theory comes to pass. As luck would have it, our teaching partnership was challenged when Dr. Bosworth won a new post at the London School of Economics, just around the time he and his partner had their first child. We accepted that our likelihood of matching a publisher's timetable was at risk. We managed the risk by accepting Palgrave's offer to divide the planned book into two, with this revised contribution moving towards publication quite a few months before the later publication of Dr. Bosworth's revised contribution.

We expect the two books to carry out a dialogue about the diversity of teaching practices appropriate for academic courses on the history of modern political thought. It is possible that Uhr and Bosworth lean in opposite directions when teaching the history of modern political theory, with Uhr tending towards the interpretative school identified by Saxonhouse as 'instrumentalist' and Bosworth tending towards the school Saxonhouse identified as 'contextualist'. It is also possible that the teaching of political theory benefits from this type of dialogue and debate over the instruments of interpretation.

I have to thank the School of Politics and International Relations at the Australian National University and the important assistance of its head, Dr. Andrew Banfield, who arranged the teaching collaboration which significantly benefited the two university academics. I also have to thank the many students at the Australian National University who enrolled in our course (officially called 'Ideas in Politics') and gave us their experience used so prominently in this book. I also want to thank the Australian Research Council for its award of a research grant on 'Australian Political Rhetoric' (DP130104628) which has led to this related research on the rhetoric of modern political theory.

My 2015 Palgrave book *Prudential Public Leadership* examined many aspects of political rhetoric, from theories originally devised by Aristotle to later refinements developed by the great British philosopher J. S. Mill and the great British statesman William Gladstone (Uhr 2015). That book was supported by the two outstanding editors of the Palgrave 'Recovering Political Philosophy' series: Thomas Pangle and Timothy

Burns, to whom I owe thanks as their inspiring research have guided this later book. The 2017 Palgrave book I co-authored with another ANU colleague, Dr. Adam Masters, is also relevant as a companion study in political rhetoric and reflection. *Leadership Performance and Rhetoric* was supported with flair by Palgrave's two assessors: Dennis Grube of Cambridge University and Robert Faulkner of Boston College (Masters and Uhr 2017). The chapters of that book examining the contribution of English philosopher Francis Bacon to the study of leadership are relevant to this book's recovery of another English philosopher—Lord Shaftesbury—who stands out as a model of the kind of academic teaching Dr. Bosworth and I later discovered we were in many respects imitating.

My debts are considerable to the anonymous reviewers commissioned by Palgrave at an early stage in the writing of this book. They will see how impressively helpful their comments have been to the later writing of this book. I also owe many thanks to the Palgrave commissioning editor Vishal Daryanomel based in Singapore, and fellow editor Anushangi Weerakoon, who have managed this book's publication with professional skill. Karen Clark's index is brief but very useful. Finally, I again thank my immediate family of Joan and Elizabeth for their endless love, their enthusiasm for spirited debate over politics and political leadership, and their support for a husband and father who, as a retiring academic, never appears quite ready to retire.

Canberra, Australia   John Uhr

References

Bailey, Andrew, et al. 2012. *The Broadview Anthology of Social and Political Thought: Essential Readings*. Peterborough, ON: Broadview Press.
Masters, Adam, and John Uhr. 2017. *Leadership Performance and Rhetoric*. London: Palgrave.
Saxonhouse, Arlene. 1988. Of Paradigms and Cores. *Polity* 21 (2): 409–418.
Saxonhouse, Arlene. 1993. Texts and Canons: The Status of Great Books in Political Theory. In *The State of the Discipline*, ed. Ada Finifter, 3–26. Washington, DC: APSA.
Saxonhouse, Arlene. 2008. Exile and Re-entry: Political Theory Yesterday and Tomorrow. In *Oxford Handbook of Political Theory*, ed. John Dryzek, Bonnie Honig, and Anne Phillips, 844–858. Oxford: Oxford University Press.
Uhr, John. 2015. *Prudential Public Leadership*. New York: Palgrave.

The original version of the book was revised: Belated corrections from author have been incorporated. The erratum to the book is available at https://doi.org/10.1007/978-981-10-7998-6_8

Contents

1 Introduction: Politics and Pedagogy   1

2 Reading Dewey   19

3 Reading Shaftesbury   33

4 Reading Machiavelli's *The Prince*   51

5 Reading J. S. Mill's *On Liberty*   69

6 Reading Nietzsche's *On the Genealogy of Morals*   85

7 Conclusion: Reading Collingwood   101

Erratum to: Performing Political Theory   E1

Index   119

CHAPTER 1

Introduction: Politics and Pedagogy

Performing as a Teacher

Abstract International political science literature shows very little guidance on how to teach the history of modern political theory. My thesis is that the great writers whose texts comprise these courses provide the best guidance: I argue that they took pedagogy seriously, with their texts intended to educate a new world of readers and followers. These theorists were performers, intending to make readers also perform as they put into practice the theories sketched in the core texts. Teachers must now be performers, helping students learn to read and think like political theorists.

Keywords History of modern political thought · Teaching performance · Writing performance · Reading performance

Performing Political Theory is a book on political education, with case studies of outstanding political theorists as educational performers—writing classic texts to stimulate readers and students to think politically. The phrase 'performing political theory' refers to the performative art of writing used by our sample set of political theorists: where 'performative' means practising the arts of 'political theory' with readers of the text.

The original version of this chapter was revised: Belated author correction has been corrected. The erratum to this chapter is available at https://doi.org/10.1007/978-981-10-7998-6_8

© The Author(s) 2018
J. Uhr, *Performing Political Theory*,
https://doi.org/10.1007/978-981-10-7998-6_1

The writers of certain political theory texts do far more than 'inform' readers about the nature of politics; these very gifted writers 'perform' theories of politics to stimulate readers to think and act theoretically when they act politically. *Performing Political Theory* shows how academic teachers can interpret complex works of political theory written by highly regarded philosophers to help readers and students participate in this important but seriously understudied form of political education.

The Promise of Performance

The title of the book refers to performing a way of thinking called 'political theory'. Academic teaching in the field of political theory helps students understand the great effort of the most influential political theorists who have shaped the history of modern political thought: Machiavelli stands at the front of this queue, with academic teachers trying as best they can to bring students to come to grips with the thinking associated with this great writer. The book title thus refers primarily to the performance of great theorists like Machiavelli whose written works flesh out theories about the nature of politics. The title, however, also refers in less direct ways to the performance of students who can be taught to appreciate the strengths and limitations of the theories of Machiavelli and his successors; and also to the performance of academic teachers whose pedagogy (or teaching practice) builds the bridge of accessibility between the writers of the past and the students of the present. This book is written by an experienced academic teacher (still learning much about pedagogy) to help others reflect on the pedagogy of bridge-building in political science education. This chapter examines the performance of the pedagogue in helping students better understand (even if they then reject their views) the great performance of some of the greatest political theorists in the modern era.

Many political scientists know the important role of US philosopher Judith Butler in mobilising research interest in *performance studies* of contemporary politics. Her first book was on 'Hegelian reflections' in French political thinking and practice, indicating Butler's unusual combination of abstract theory and challenging political practice. A later book closer to what we think of as performance studies was called *Excitable Speech* with a subtitle on 'a politics of the performative'. Another book in 2015 examined 'a performative theory of assembly' referring to what groups of people do when they perform together, assembled to defend or promote whatever interests they consider of social importance in their role as designated public officials or simply as activist citizens (Butler 2015). Of more immediate interest here is the background influence of British philosopher J. L. Austin (1911–1960) who is generally regarded as the founder of contemporary performance studies because of his influential, if quietly methodical, examination of speech acts—including 'performative utterances' (Austin 2001). Evaluations of the many schools of performance studies affecting contemporary politics would have to begin with Butler's considerable work compared to very many additional later schools of analysis. Here the task is more modest and retrospective; it is to look back at Austin's original reflections on 'performance utterances' setting the stage for our own recovery of earlier historical examples of political theory conceived of performatively.

Much turns on differences between *informing* and *performing*. Austin was trying to identify a form of speech act which differed from those that were informative. His hope was that he could defend something important about 'ordinary language' not well understood in the specialisms of speech analysis in twentieth-century philosophy. His focus was on types of speech used 'not to report facts but to influence people in this way or that'. Some of his examples are from the bottom up: of people, including self-interested schemers, pleading for special treatment. Other examples are from the top down: of people exercising some kind of public authority, which might be fair and reasonable or might be unfair and false. This distinction between performances that are fair or unfair implies that not all performances are credible. On some occasions, we might be 'not entirely responsible for doing what we are doing'; or indeed we could be 'acting a play or making a joke' for some particular reason, so that 'we shall not be able to say that we seriously performed the act concerned'. Of relevance here is Austin's own rather abbreviated explanation of what distinguishes an appropriate from an inappropriate exercise of performative speech. Defending the ritual of performative speech, Austin generally relies on common sense or conventional explanation of what society might hold as appropriate or inappropriate exercises of performative speech. Hence it might be thought appropriate for judges to determine hard or soft sentences but it might be held inappropriate for police officers to deal with lawbreakers firmly or softly (Austin 2001, 1435; see also Rosen 2002, 182–193).

Austin's claim was that what he termed 'performance utterances' shaped rather than reflected a state of affairs. Put otherwise, these types of performance prescribed rather than described a state of affairs. A judge who sentences a convicted person is *enscribing* rather than *describing* that sentence—which comes into existence precisely because of the judge's performance when judging. Speech or text which functions as performance is not merely saying something but is *doing* something: the speech or text performs the action it addresses. Austin acknowledged that his formulation might allow sceptics to warn us of loopholes where 'perjurers and welshers' could claim to have performed or nor performed simply on the basis of cleverly persuasive rhetoric. But his larger point was that performative speech was inevitably rhetorical. Claiming that performative speech 'must be appropriate to its invocation', Austin allowed that performative utterances exercised an element of what he awkwardly—or 'rather hurriedly' as he writes—called 'the notion of forces of utterances'. Force here means persuasion where the performer speaks acceptably to audiences in ways that fall outside the categories of true or false required of nonperformative statements. Austin invites his readers to accept the implication that performative language is rhetorical—although very little in Austin's own analysis acknowledges in what ways rhetoric may be fair and reasonable or unfair and false (Austin 2001, 1442; see also Rosen 2002, 193–203).

Austin's philosophy of ordinary language made special room for the ordinary practice of performative utterances. What is so attractive about Austin's restoration of this form of rhetoric is that it is believed to be ordinary rather than, so to speak, extraordinary. Yet what is less attractive is the lack of close attention to those performances worth admiring and those worth condemning. Implicit in Austin's approach is an acceptance of 'appropriate' performances and a rejection of 'inappropriate' performances. What distinguishes the appropriate from the inappropriate is, I think, underexplored. Austin refers to explanations of social convenience when audiences defer to acknowledged authorities like judges. It might well be that in these cases of worthy performance, audiences submit to the informal education as well as the formal authority of those worthy performers. Austin says little about formal or informal education as part of credible performance. Austin certainly helps us today recognise the public power of performative utterances. What we now need, however, is a more detailed examination of case studies not only of ordinary but also what we might think of as *extraordinary* exercises of performative utterances—which generate audience acceptance for their education even in the absence of formal authority. Machiavelli's cagy utterances in *The Prince* are a good example; as are Mill's wry reflections in *On Liberty*; and as are Nietzsche's revolutionary ruminations in *On the Genealogy of Morals*.

POLITICAL EDUCATION

The topic of political education is of increasing importance to contemporary democracy. The large amount of literature on 'democratic civics', however, pays very little attention to the role of political theory in civics education. The exceptions to the rule are rare. One good example—now sadly dated—is Melvin Richter's edited collection on *Political Theory and Political Education* (Richter 1980). Some of the chapters from the Richter collection illustrate educational strategies I have revisited in this book. For example, the chapters by Bernard Williams ('Political Philosophy and the Analytical Tradition'), Allan Bloom ('The Study of Texts') and J. G. A. Pocock ('Political Ideas as Historical Events: Political Philosophers as Historical Actors') all relate to the history of political thought and to the role of classic writers of key texts as not only political theorists but also as political educators. These influential students of political interpretation debate different ways we can begin to discern and evaluate 'theories' hidden in the great historical treasures of political philosophy. My aim is more modest: this book will tell a story about effective ways of teaching the history of important texts illustrating the nature of modern political thought.

Of course, the problems facing effective teaching and learning have been well known for some time. For example, Richter noted in 1980 (when commenting on Bloom's chapter) that students tended not to read much, had little training in abstract reasoning and knew very little about 'the imaginative work of the past' (Richter 1980, 32; see also Bloom 1990, 295–314). Hence this pioneering editor searched for 'pedagogical' reflections to help those academic teachers interested in cultivating an interest among students on 'how to read a great book' (Richter 1980, 35). I think this book addresses this topic from the perspective of the engaged teacher who stands between students and writers of great books in political theory. The political science profession has only a few resources likely to help academic teachers gather their bearings. Rare it is that the American Political Science Association breaks ranks and publishes as part of 'teacher symposium' an article on 'the dilemmas of teaching political theory' (Moore 2017). More typical is the reference to old and nearly forgotten books on 'the professor and the polity' where old gems like Bloom's 'Political Science and the Undergraduate' appear (Bloom 1977, 117–127). Searching in the wrong places can occasionally reveal other gems like Martin Diamond's various reviews of the study of politics in a liberal education (Diamond 1971, 6–10; see also Diamond 1977a, 89–115; 1977b, 3–21).

My aim is to demonstrate a new way of teaching the history of political thought. The aim is to encourage cautious or sceptical students to take a deeper interest in practices of political theory: reading, reflecting, discussing and debating core texts in the history of political thought. If cautious students want to remain negative about the value of old political theory texts, my plan is to help them do so in an informed way, after taking into account the rhetorical skill of these historical writers. I hope I can persuade students to take political theory seriously as a way of thinking through—or at least thinking about—many important political issues. As academics, we think that historical political thinkers can be seen to be performing politically, acting as advocates of certain types of political engagement which differ from thinker to thinker. Yet common to so many influential political theorists is a commitment to 'thinking politically' and an endeavour to present texts which can help readers and students learn to 'think politically'.

Given that this type of political thinking differs from 'thinking dogmatically', I have to warn students that many of these classic texts are edgy and experimental, challenging readers with roundabout ways of learning basic practices of critical thinking. This quality of 'roundaboutness' is political: it distracts enemies while rewarding friends. Thinkers in the historical tradition of Western political theory can think grandly as abstract philosophers, and can often write grandly abstract works of philosophy; but in other works, they can also write practically as highly skilled political performers, nudging readers towards new insights—or even old and forgotten insights—into politics.

Readers might find it hard to discern this unusual style of performance in dense books of heavy political argument. Yet there are some very useful examples, like the Strauss and Cropsey *History of Political Philosophy* (1st edition 1963; 2nd edition 1972; 3rd edition 1987), helping students—and their teachers—with 'a reading suggestion' on 'indispensable' but also optional text selections (see e.g. Strauss and Cropsey 1987, xiv). This multi-authored intellectual history tries to help by having each chapter focus on the 'abiding' or 'enduring questions' rather than simplified or potentially simplistic answers (Strauss and Cropsey 1987, xiii). The promise is that students really do need to move on from a book of commentary to confront directly the texts as written by the acknowledged experts in political thinking. My own approach is again somewhat different in that I think that academic teachers themselves can also learn how to be better lecturers—by studying the various styles of questioning adopted by historically important writers of political theory.

Reference resources like the *Journal of Political Science Education* have very few articles on the history of political theory (http://www.tandfoline.com). A rare exception is J. A. Johnson's article on models for teaching the history of political thought (Johnson 2008). Other potentially relevant sources like *Perspectives on Political Science* have a small number of relevant articles, although very few document educational practices as thoroughly as I do in this book. The most promising British source is the International Political Education Database (IPED) sponsored by the Political Studies Association, which is very comprehensive for those looking for sources on 'teaching and learning resources for politics' (http://sites.google.com/site/psatlg). Yet even in such a valuable source, it is very difficult to find resources relevant to learning about the teaching of political theory—despite IPED's generous listing of 'political theory' sources.

One of the few very good resources we have used, in the classroom and in this book, is Arlene Saxonhouse's chapter on 'Texts and Canons' (Saxonhouse 1993). This chapter examines competing approaches (notably two: followers of either Quentin Skinner or Leo Strauss) to the study of core texts in political theory, evaluating their relative strengths in helping students understand classic writings in political theory. A more recent resource is J. E. Green's essay on 'Political Theory as Both Philosophy and History', with its comparison of three competing schools of interpretation: Strauss's supposed 'didactic' school; Skinner's 'historicist' school; and Habermas's 'critical-rational' school (Green 2015). I tend to follow Green's defence of being 'at home amongst the classics' against the challenges posed by what he terms analytical and historicist approaches to political theory which are uncomfortable when called on to 'shepherd the classics'. In ways unexplored by Green, I accept his description that academic teachers of political theory are 'human bridges' linking students to historical 'classics' (Green 2015, 439).

These examples are exceptions. The result of the limited attention to 'theory teaching' is that students can find it almost impossible to grant historical writers the status of performers. Despite this, I think that this book's view of the performative element of political theory can strengthen academic courses in the history of political thought. With colleagues at the Australian National University, I have been teaching and experimenting with a core course in the history of modern political thought highlighting the *drama* of political theory—based on the evidence of key historical theorists as deliberately and carefully *performing* the texts students are expected to study. Our intention has been 'to build a better bridge' between the two intellectual communities we as academic teachers try to relate: the talented but sceptical community of students required to study history of political thought; and the 'source material' composed by historically important intellects whose key texts survive as baffling challenges to easy comprehension.

Our bridge is built around our teaching practice. Our role as academic lecturers means that we stand between the students and the theorists about to be studied. Our claim is that many of the core political theorists are themselves bridge-builders, in the sense that they 'practice political theory' through their craft of communication. 'Performing political theory' thus refers to the style and mode of public communication: that is, choices about the 'form' of arguments in a text of political theory shape the ways the audience is 'in-formed'. We try to help students begin to see theorists as a special kind of public performer—each with their own choice of what they see as their relevant rhetoric as an essential means to promote the ends of their favoured theory of politics.

Our experiment in academic teaching reinforces this creative bridge-building when we help students interpret the classical texts by learning to see not only the valuable *craft* of the core texts but also the often neglected or ignored *stagecraft* of selected theorists. This book illustrates our approach to teaching political theory through a set of case studies examining different forms of performance carried out by the rhetorics of communication used in so many different ways by many very influential political theorists. I do not pretend that political theory can be reduced to one common set of rhetorical rituals; instead, I think that three core theorists (Machiavelli, Mill and Nietzsche) differ quite significantly in their rhetorical performances—with each using a distinctive mode of public communication designed to promote a particular type of theory of politics.

There are likely to be many styles of theoretical 'performance'. This book examines interesting examples of modern political thought which are variations on this theme: thought as represented in selected texts from these three writers. What is common to all theorists is their 'publicity'. In contrast to other theorists who might have avoided 'going public' in order to protect their version of theory from unwanted intrusion or external misunderstanding, these three theorists went on the public record to promote their practice of political theory. Presumably, all knew that political theory was a minority practice of interest mainly to public intellectuals and their networks of political influence. Thus, it would be a surprise to find any of these three acting like a head of a political movement or a political leader in conventional politics. Yet all three went out of their way to engage in public debate over very significant political themes; one (J. S. Mill) even went into parliamentary politics to conserve or progress political doctrines led by others.

THE RHETORIC OF PERFORMANCE

Contemporary uses of the term 'performance' and 'performativity' reflect interests in the rhetoric at work when public figures engage with audiences when carrying out their public roles. Performances are activities that are not simply acted but are, to use contemporary language, 'enacted'. By extension to this topic of political theory, the theorist might act as the writer of a work of theory (e.g. Machiavelli's *The Prince*) but the deeper performance occurs when that theory is 'enacted'—that is, when an audience of readers is persuaded to think like Machiavelli thinks of politics, even if only to reject or qualify Machiavelli's perspective on politics. The first task is not deciding for or against Machiavelli, which almost all readers eventually do quite quickly; the first task is striving to understand Machiavelli's political theory as it was understood by Machiavelli. We can try to make that task as simple as possible by confining our evidence to only one of Machiavelli's many written texts, such as *The Prince*. Yet even this one small text is hard to interpret—hard to put it into practice, which is one way of making sense of a political theory. The performance of the theorist Machiavelli is making the text of *The Prince* 'enactable', by which we mean open to interpretative 'interactivity' (to use contemporary academic language) among his community of readers. This cumbersome term 'enactable' does not mean 'applicable' as though the work written by the theorist could be readily implemented by its readers. As we will see in the later chapter on *The Prince*, this political theory text is quite a performance because it asks a lot of its readers—if they really do want to learn to think like Machiavelli. The writer knew that readers would have to learn to read critically if they were to learn to think theoretically. The text resembles the script of play, with the writer-theorist nudging readers to take into account all the characters competing for our attention—including the character of the author.

In many contemporary schools of performance studies, a performance is a complex cultural practice often considered as an alternative to a 'text'. My approach brings back the 'text' although in a new way. Traditional approaches might be thought to have isolated 'theory' to space inside the 'text', with the implication that understanding a writer's theory meant folding oneself back into the 'text', inspired by a kind of 'textualism' where everything theoretical was 'in the text' and the appropriate interpretative discipline was this reverential 'textualism'. My approach sees the theorist-writer as a very special kind of intellectual performer whose work of theory is really a work of great art demanding something interactive of its readers. Machiavelli's *The Prince* contains the germs of his political theory which is available to readers who are prepared to participate in the type of performance expected by Machiavelli—who, as we shall see later in this book, scripted his work of theory so that it is best interpreted by those who read as carefully, and as radically, as Machiavelli wrote. The theoretical text we know as *The Prince* is in many respects a play prepared by its author to engage and educate the deepest curiosities of its readers. Thinking theoretically then becomes an exercise in 'reading the rhetoric' as constructively composed and cleverly arranged by the theorist Machiavelli.

By 'rhetoric', I here mean rhetoric in its most simple form as the use of arts of persuasion, with performers making choices about which types of persuasive evidence (*logos* or *ethos* or *pathos* or some combination of all three, to use Aristotle's categories) will work with audiences (Aristotle 2007). I am not applying any specific theory or concept of 'performance' prominent in contemporary academic discourse, so readers should not expect to find here 'an application' of a current performance theory to a particular field of political activity. Common to most schools of performance studies is recognition that performance is a form of rhetoric where performers see their task as persuading audiences through various rhetorical activities intended to cultivate agreement or acceptance by audiences with work or policy promoted by performers. The importance of rhetoric in studies of performance highlights a key feature of the widely used term 'performance': this is the recognition that 'performers' use 'audiences' to enact or implement their schemes. Audiences, in turn, also 'perform' in the ways they watch, attend to and listen to staged activities. Beyond the stage, as it were, audiences mobilise and shape user reception; and towards the stage, as it were, audiences react positively or negatively to actors' initiation. Thus, the interaction (or 'interactivity') between actors and audiences define the public performance we can then study or admire or dislike—as part of our own academic performance.

Performance relates to the interaction or communication between what we might broadly term composers and consumers. True, in many cases, composers perform among themselves, turning original 'texts' into performative works accessible to audiences—as written works of music become publicly accessible entertainments. So too, consumers also work among themselves, with privileged early onlookers (e.g. book or film reviewers) activating later audiences to engage with or ignore composers' performances. Each step in the link of performances involves decisions about rhetoric, with choices made about what forms of information (logical or ethical or pathetic, to use again categories from Aristotle) might help persuade audiences about the strengths or weaknesses of performative works. Across the mass of scholarly studies of performance, these two elements of audience and rhetoric feature prominently: sometimes minimally, and at other times more forcefully, performers use many arts of rhetoric to engage with audiences.

Foreshadowing Shaftesbury

My orientation does not derive from any particular contemporary school of performance studies. Instead, I will recover earlier notions of performance formulated by Lord Shaftesbury (1671–1713) whose contribution to political theory usually passes unnoticed. Shaftesbury was initially a member of the House of Commons and later the House of Lords. He was the grandson of one of the architects of the Glorious Revolution of 1689 which moderated the powers of the British monarchy and ushered in a regime of parliamentary government. Shaftesbury was tutored by a very great political philosopher, John Locke. He was deeply immersed in the politics of his day; yet he was also a thinker and writer of promise. His vast volume called *Characteristics* includes as one of its component books a work called *Soliloquy, or Advice to an Author* (Shaftesbury 1999, 70–162). This strange work is part of the set of works by Shaftesbury which has had such a great influence on European philosophies of fine art. Of interest to this project is Shaftesbury's remarkable innovation of the role of 'performance' in social and political thought.

In many respects, Shaftesbury is a neglected founder of performance studies. Three elements of his theory of performance are relevant to this book. First, Shaftesbury recognised that great writers are great performers and that our understanding of their works requires that we as readers watch and assess this performative relationship between writer and reader. Understanding great works of writing means learning to read their specific types of rhetoric used by so many writers to transport their works of art. Shaftesbury is a pioneer in the study of 'style' which should feature more prominently in the contemporary study of political theory. Shaftesbury forces us to pay close attention to 'the style' of written texts by great political theorists. Second, audiences look to writers not simply for entertainment but for instruction, especially instruction in the nature of the virtues through which we as social beings are likely to develop our sense of humanity. Shaftesbury is a virtue theorist of the highest importance: part of his careful relationship with John Locke reflected his opposition to Locke's strategy of liberal individualism which appeared to Shaftesbury to undermine many important civic virtues required by modern political systems. One of the neglected virtues recovered by Shaftesbury is a practical reason or prudence—including the skills of prudence used in reading works of intellectual merit exploring the civic nature of politics. Third, the realm between writers and readers calls for a new activity of 'criticism' managed by a new set of 'critics' who help readers appreciate the real arts of great writers. Shaftesbury stands out as a model of the type of literary critic he himself did so much to develop as a social role or indeed as a civic office. Shaftesbury's *Soliloquy* makes the case for the critic and for criticism in ways that make it the very model for the type of intelligent bridge-building between text and student that academic instructors aim to construct. There is more to come on Shaftesbury in Chapter 3.

Teaching Practice

Generally, what is it that this set of prominent theorists—Machiavelli, Mill and Nietzsche—thought they were doing when they so openly circulated their preferred theories of politics? My answer relates to their status as 'classics' in political theory: these authors saw themselves as 'classifiers' of theories or philosophies of politics, and saw their works as exemplars of the practice of the valuable—but vulnerable—minority arts of political theory or philosophy. Their welcome public role in 'performing' political theory is evident in their remarkably dissimilar texts, each of which reflects the author's judgment about how best to put on public display the practice of this kind of political philosophy. It is possible that one or more of this set of three authors had low expectations about the possibility of genuine public understanding of theory or philosophy; hence it is possible that some of them might have modified or 'softened' some of the more demanding aspects of their own philosophical practice. In works of political theory, these authors might have acted politically as well as philosophically—presenting a simplified version of their deeper philosophical beliefs located in other works not intended for widespread public attention.

As academic lecturers, our interest has been in the role of the theorists as educators. Sensing that writers act as bridge-builders, I have emphasised to students the many ways that great theorists 'put on show' great ways of thinking about politics. Their performances are exercises in helping interested readers to learn how to think theoretically—and to act with a committed sense of justice informed by that theory. In our view, our theorists want their readers to begin to perform more theoretically by following the pathways outlined in their texts. The odd complexity of these core texts reflects the depth of ambition of each author to shape a new public philosophy around the new public philosophers formed by their instructive works. Each of the three authors wrote many credible public works of political theory: in this book, I examine one example from each theorist to help students see that taking political theory seriously means taking these texts more as 'mind games' than revelations of the deepest core concepts about the nature of politics.

Examples can help. Analysts of the history of modern political thought often assume that the classic core texts share an interest in concepts of 'the state'. Thus much of the commentary on figures like Hobbes or Locke turns on 'the architecture of the state': trying to determine how these theorists might want their followers to apply their 'theory' through some sort of application of specified institutions. This state-centred approach has much to recommend it, and it resembles the way many contemporary commentators on an influential theorist like John Rawls debate which type of institutions best apply Rawls' theory to concrete practice. But my interest is slightly different, because I think students can get deeper into the world of political theory by studying the intellectual *process* as well as the institutional *substance* of political theory. Machiavelli is at the head of our list and I think he fits the bill well because in *The Prince* he does what a good orator does: he walks the audience around the subject matter so that they begin to accept some perspectives while they distant themselves from other perspectives.

The influential scholar Viroli has documented Machiavelli's characteristic writing performance in his *Redeeming the Prince* (Viroli 2014). I think this shows that Machiavelli's 'teaching' is closer to the *drama* of his cut and thrust writing than to any conclusive *doctrine* readers might expect from him. Learning to think like Machiavelli might mean learning to resist conclusive doctrines or simplified solutions.

Another example of a politically performative theorist is Kant. We know that he is about as grandly theoretical as theorists can get, so that it is certainly possible to study Kant in order to learn what a perfectly abstract world of politics might look like. But I use a different approach. I acknowledge that students can read a text like Kant's *Perpetual Peace* to envisage how institutions like republicanism, federalism and cosmopolitanism might be applied to politics. But I invite students to read this text to learn more about Kant's way of performing political theory. Partly following my earlier interpretation of Kant as a profound educator (Uhr 2015, 103–123), I see Kant's performance in a work like *Perpetual Peace* as 'cultivating Kantians': learning political theory from Kant means learning to think like Kant, or more specifically, to think along the lines developed by Kant in his performance in this classic text. Kant might well have reserved for other times or other places his more deeply considered philosophical beliefs. Yet it is still possible that such a deep thinker could have used *Perpetual Peace* for a different, possibly more preliminary, purpose of political education.

Our sample set of theorists begins with Machiavelli and ends with Nietzsche. Both of these political theorists had concepts of the state but my attention is taken by their similar interest in political education. *The Prince* does not map out a model constitution and the *Genealogy of Morals* falls short of theorising what a comprehensive moral code might look like. But both these influential theorists saw their potential influence to come from cultivating readers who could learn to perform theoretically as followers of either Machiavelli or Nietzsche. In my approach, students are then encouraged to take a closer look at high-range political theory by learning to think like these authors—or at least to think along the lines sketched out in public in the classic texts by these political theorists.

The book's case studies put this educational model to the test. My teaching experience has convinced me that students can learn more about the nature of political theory when they begin to see theorists as performers and their core texts as 'scripts' meant to play out actively in the drama of public deliberation. My approach is *elitist* to the extent that so many great political theorists saw their public role as shapers of public sentiment through their contribution to political debate and dialogue. But this approach is also *democratic* to the extent that the performance of political theory resembles a public competition where no theorist can ever really be confident that the political community will ever properly comprehend the content of their theory or rally to their support as welcome partisans. The result is fiery contest over the nature of 'the political' by fierce champions of very deep thought conveyed often in deceptively persuasive written argument.

My approach is practical as a guide to teachers and students of political theory. In this book, I am not uncovering new truths about the core teachings of the writers we examine. I am making the best case from readily available editions of well-known texts, with no pretence about comprehensive new understanding drawn from lost or minor or forgotten works. My aim is put our task to a practical test by using a typical sourcebook familiar to students. The aim is to show how university teachers can use conventional materials in unconventional ways, so that students can learn to value political theory as a 'performance practice' as revealed in the fascinatingly different performances worked out by our set of three core theorists. Here the aim is to help teachers and students in a more practical task, which is 'bridging the gap' between students and texts in political theory—and allowing students at a later date to step up to the higher task of taking the texts in their full complexity as complete and finished works of philosophy.

Preview of Sample Theorists

Machiavelli's *The Prince* is often seen as something of a crafty 'oration' (Viroli 2014). I can show some of the ways that Machiavelli coached his audience in the arts of performance. The rhetoric of *The Prince* carries readers through an amazing political landscape containing many examples of different types of rule. Machiavelli resembles a ruler in using his writing to 'rule in' and 'rule out' certain types of conduct. His text appears ambiguous or even confused to many readers; but I show that Machiavelli is using many of these contradictions to loosen up his audience so that his more astute readers can begin to disconnect from conventional authority and to chart their own way around this political landscape. *The Prince* opens with a dedication to ruling authority and ends with an exhortation to national liberation. In between, the text bristles with carefully crafted confusion. Readers can respond by slowly becoming more 'Machiavellian' as they try to piece together whole cloth out of the colourful fragments presented by Machiavelli.

Mill's *On Liberty* is the subject of endless debate over 'the two Mills', with champions of the libertarian Mill debating their interpretations of individuality with champions of the socialistic Mill with their interpretations of sociality. My approach opens up a new path by revealing what I take to be Mill's deeper interest in virtue or excellence which sometimes can take the form of individual preference and at other times the form of social duty. My examination reveals Mill's work as an exercise in public advocacy designed to promote liberties supportive of civic virtue. Mill's five chapters are nudges for and against conventional styles of liberty, with the author attempting to 'liberalise' readers to see a new interrelationship between individual and civic virtue. Mill is neither the radical individualist nor the naïve socialist many claim him to be.

Nietzsche's *The Genealogy of Morals* seems to fit back into the performance mould we discovered in Machiavelli. Students find Nietzsche a burdensome thinker: and part of this reputation comes from their reluctance to think of him as a public performer. Students do not know how to read Nietzsche and in many ways Nietzsche encourages this uncertainty. But my approach helps students move their attention from the apparent welfare of slave morality to the potential revolution of master morality. Nietzsche's laboured contrast appears too colourful and simplistic, until students begin to see that this contrast is only a pathway to a richer understanding of the unnoticed weights of modern progress and the difficult but slowly discernible liberations of what we now term 'postmodernity' which this text slowly clarifies. This proponent of postmodernism uses the *Genealogy* to look backwards to trace the development of rival spirits of politics: going beyond modernity means going backward to recover lost disciplines through which 'great politics' can be relaunched.

Conclusion

I see political theory as one important mode of political activity. I concede that theorists can engage in many types of politics: some progressive, some conservative, with many conventionally liberal in the period of modern political history we are covering. To see political theorists as performing politically means that I am recognising their writing as a form of politics. One of our sources for this view is Claude Lefort whose *Writing* elaborates many ways that writers can use texts to promote styles of thinking which expand on or even at times escape from their texts (Lefort 2000). I have more to say on Lefort in the following chapter. Lefort sees many theoretical writers as performers who decompose conventional certainties and recompose unconventional thinking. While Machiavelli is one of his examples (Lefort 2000, 109–141), I think important claims can also be made about our other influential political theorists, each of whom wrote works designed to keep us thinking about the nature of politics long after any resolution of contending debates about core concepts in politics and governance. This is not a book solely of political history but a book of political education, using historical examples as evidence about a way of teaching texts to convey the inviting nature of political theory. I think that certain performative writers can promote political theory as an academic activity students and teachers should be invited to share.

References

Aristotle. 2007. *On Rhetoric: A Theory of Civic Discourse,* trans. George A. Kennedy, 2nd ed. New York: Oxford University Press.

Austin, J.L. 2001. Performative Utterances. In *The Norton Anthology of Theory and Criticism,* ed. Vincent B. Leith, 1430–1442. New York: Norton and Company.

Bloom, Allan. 1977. Political Science and the Undergraduate, Chap. 6. In *Teaching Political Science: The Professor and the Polity,* ed. Vernon Van Dyke, 117–127. Highland, NJ: Humanities Press.

Bloom, Allan. 1990. The Study of Texts. In *Giants and Dwarfs: Essays 1960–1990,* 295–314. New York: Simon and Schuster.

Butler, Judith. 2015. *Notes Towards a Performative Theory of Assembly.* Cambridge: Harvard University Press.

Diamond, Martin. 1971. On the Study of Politics in a Liberal Education. *The College* (December) 22 (4): 6–10.

Diamond, Martin. 1977a. Teaching of Political Science as a Vocation. In *Teaching Political Science,* ed. Vernon Van Dyke, 89–115. Highland, NJ: Humanities Press.

Diamond, Martin. 1977b. Teaching About Politics as a Vocation. In *The Ethics of Teaching and Scientific Research,* ed. Sidney Hook et al., 3–21. Amherst, NY: Prometheus.

Green, J.E. 2015. Political Theory as Both Philosophy and History. *Annual Review of Political Science* 18: 425–441.

Johnson, J.A. 2008. On the Advantage and Disadvantage of History for Teaching Political Theory to Undergraduates. *Journal of Political Science Education* 4 (3): 341–356.

Lefort, Claude. 2000. *Writing: The Political Test*. Durham: Duke University Press.

Moore, Matthew J. 2017. Textbooks and the Dilemmas of Teaching Political Theory. *PS: Political Science & Politics* 50 (2): 531–535.

Richter, Melvin. 1980. *Political Theory and Political Education*. Princeton: Princeton University Press.

Rosen, Stanley. 2002. Austin and Ordinary Language, Chap. 6. In *The Elusiveness of the Ordinary*, 182–203. New Haven: Yale University Press.

Saxonhouse, Arlene. 1993. Texts and Canons. In *The State of the Discipline*, ed. Ada Finifter, 2–26. Washington, DC: APSA.

Shaftesbury, Lord. 1999. Soliloquy. In *Characteristics*, ed. L.E. Klein, 70–162. Cambridge: Cambridge University Press.

Strauss, Leo, and Joseph Cropsey. 1987. Preface to the First Edition. In *History of Political Philosophy*, 3rd ed., xiii–xiv. Chicago: University of Chicago Press.

Uhr, John. 2015. *Prudential Public Leadership*. New York: Palgrave.

Viroli, Maurizio. 2014. *Redeeming the Prince*. Princeton: Princeton University Press.

CHAPTER 2

Reading Dewey

Performing as a Writer

Abstract The first lesson comes from US philosopher John Dewey who knew how important education was to modern democracy. Dewey's narrative of the history of modern political thought highlights the educational power of pioneers of modernity like Francis Bacon and others who wrote works to re-educate readers for the promotion of modernity.

Keywords John Dewey · Modernity · Pedagogy · Education

This is a book about pedagogy and modern political theory. The core of the book has several case studies revealing a pedagogy used when teaching the history of modern political thought. The interesting puzzle is that the story of pedagogy does not stop there: I reveal how several leading theorists of modern politics (Machiavelli, Mill and Nietzsche) were also involved in pedagogy as they shaped their written works to communicate new theories about thinking and acting politically. The form of the book is educational rather than philosophical or even political: I argue that each of the leading theorists here examined took seriously their role as public educators, writing their ambitious works of political theory in unusually fascinating ways intended to attract something

---

The original version of this chapter was revised: Belated author corrections have been corrected. The erratum to this chapter is available at https://doi.org/10.1007/978-981-10-7998-6_8

© The Author(s) 2018
J. Uhr, *Performing Political Theory*,
https://doi.org/10.1007/978-981-10-7998-6_2

of a political community, possibly even a political following, among those readers they could persuade to commit to their political theory.

This chapter uses John Dewey (1859–1952) to highlight the case about the educational interests of great philosophers shaping modernity. The philosopher Dewey is something of an expert witness who can verify the credibility of those who view great philosophical writers as engaged in a special type of public pedagogy. Dewey says little about Machiavelli or Mill or Nietzsche as educational modernisers, but he says much about modernisation which is the process of historical development shaping so much of the work of these three political theorists. Each of these three theorists takes their orientation from the Enlightenment: Machiavelli to nudge it open, Mill to focus it on excellence, and Nietzsche to reform it to protect aspects of greatness lost under the march of modernisation. Dewey articulates the political philosophy of the Enlightenment by noting the neglected cultivation of pedagogy in the otherwise specialist or expert doctrines of innovation marshalled by Enlightenment thinkers (Fott 2009).

Dewey's history of philosophy reveals important examples of political theory at work modernising the world. Francis Bacon's belief in the Enlightenment was based on a hope that progressive science could be managed for a worthy public purpose—with natural science serving as an instrument of political justice by giving us the power to use 'for the relief of man's estate'. Dewey shares this Enlightenment model of wholesale political reform to use the power of the mind to reform the power of government, even to the point of having systems of government serve a liberating public goal—with representative government tending in the direction of popular government. Dewey's history paints the heroic past in fascinating colours not always used by his Baconian heroes, as he encourages us to see potential democracy informed by modern liberalism pushing away from traditional regimes of despotism. My use of Dewey's philosophy of history may strike some readers as softheaded, because readers will know that contemporary systems of liberal democracy have never lived up to the highest expectations articulated in Dewey's democratic political theory. My reply is that Dewey remains valuable for my study of pedagogy in political theory, precisely because those who know best his social and political philosophy also know that his historical interpretation of the public influence of great philosophical writers documents the pedagogic power of these gifted writers who transformed the public sphere in directions favourable to their readers and those who would become sovereign in modern democracy (see e.g. Stuhr 1998).

Writers and Readers

Even those readers who are suspicious or distrustful of great political theorists have to begin their disengagement with an initial engagement: critical readers have to try to see things in the light of the advocate they suspect will eventually fail to persuade them of the merits of their theory. There are very simple alternatives, such as not bothering to read all that much by theorists who appear distrustful or are reputed to be distrustful, or simply assuming that theorists with the 'wrong' theories are looking for lackeys through the clever use of sophistic rhetoric. Simple solutions create their own problems, especially if new readers to a political theorist fear that trying to see things as they were originally seen by this or any other theorist means we 'fall in' with the dim-witted lackeys who become the followers for yet another scheming intellectual leader.

One of the advantages which will come from our close reading of a few of the core texts of some of the greatest political theorists is that we will see that each of the theorists feared lackadaisical followers and so wrote their works of political theory in carefully indirect ways. To understand these theorist as they understood themselves means coming to terms with their cagy rhetoric intended to carve out a following free from the lazy bluster of intellectual lackeys. As we shall see, they wrote for a special type of audience of 'critics' perhaps first appreciated by Shaftesbury, as will be examined in chapter three: critics who could follow the rhetoric of presentation as framed by these writers who preferred cultivating critical friends rather than the type of feeble followers many contemporary interpreters warn us to avoid.

This chapter draws on the intellectual history established by Dewey. Dewey's general themes are democracy and education, so we find in his intellectual history a narrative of educational innovation pioneered by a number of very great political philosophers. Dewey's historical narrative helps us recover the educational performance of these great writers, of whom English philosopher Francis Bacon is probably a classic type (Dewey 1966, 61–68). In Dewey's story, the performance of a philosophical writer relates to their educational innovation of using their own texts as educational sources for the critical readers they cultivated—critical readers who could assimilate the progressive tendencies scattered within the rhetorical complexities of these texts as they worked in a partnership with their chosen authors to become public educators ready to play a political role in the manner best described in Shaftesbury's account of 'criticism'.

The preferred models of political thinking vary considerably among great political thinkers, as the case studies note. But common to all cases of writing about politics is this interest in educational public communication: in effect, a rhetoric of public instruction. Studies of rhetoric in political theory tend to focus on what I might term the 'inner rhetorics' of intellectual argument as distinct from what I term the 'outer rhetorics' of public persuasion. My project is to approach the inner world of core argument through the outer world of public presentation, guided as far as possible by the arts of writing used by our sample of great thinkers. To put it crudely: composition cues us to comprehension. Our sample of outstanding shapers of modern political thought was convinced that they could educate readers in new ways of thinking and acting politically. This focus on newness meant that these thinkers knew that their task was not conservative: they were not reinforcing or entrenching established or conventional views about politics, but instead innovating new ways of revising or refining or reforming or re-evaluating traditional ways of reading politics.

I admit that my focus on the educational rhetoric or pedagogy is unusual in contemporary political theory. The standard practice is to worry less about the arts of public communication and to engage more with the core substantive content of the political theories devised by each great theorist. Students of rhetoric might be interested in the styles of communication adopted by leading political thinkers but students of political theory are more often interested in the *thoughts* which are partly seen, and also partly hidden, in the cumbersome arrangement of *words* assembled by these great thinkers. I too am also closely interested in the thoughts of these key thinkers. I think that, in many cases, their thoughts related to their rhetorical responsibilities in the public communication of their reflections on politics. My case studies try to show that each of our featured thinkers reflected very seriously on the nature of their writing as a contribution to the greater public understanding of the nature of politics.

I accept that for many premodern thinkers, this kind of reflection might well have cautioned them against high hopes for a greater public understanding of politics or political philosophy. So too, later antimodern thinkers might have locked away many of their thoughts from public scrutiny. But my selection begins with Machiavelli who in so many ways typifies the style of writing and communication of the moderns (and modernisers) I examine—all of whom, including the conservative or reactionary philosophies favoured by Nietzsche, sought to promote a solid public doctrine around their chosen themes of politics. My set of 'Machiavellians' are modernisers searching for a preferred public doctrine of modernity fit for communication to those readers ready and able enough to decipher the written words of political theory and to share the theories shaped and circulated by these, and indeed many other, influential political thinkers.

Dewey's Political Pedagogy

My focus on the pedagogies of political theory should come as no surprise to readers and students of Dewey who is an important authority on procedure and process in politics and policy. He is also an expert on pedagogy. Procedure and pedagogy are both important elements of Dewey's model of democracy: for Dewey, democratic public leadership works through procedures of checks and balances, and democratic political education has a pedagogy which uses checks and balances to restrain the controlling power of leaders and to train the supportive power of followers. Dewey's own leadership in intellectual history has encouraged me to rediscover the political pedagogy used by influential political thinkers who fit the type celebrated in Dewey's history of modernising philosophers shaping our contemporary world of democracy.

Part of Dewey's framework is evident in his *Democracy and Education* (originally published in 1916) where democracy is recognised as a 'conjoint communicated experience' nurtured by public intellectuals with a gift for public communication (Dewey 1966, 87). Proponents of modern democracy have long shared a programme of using their public power as writers and publicists to emancipate peoples 'from the internal chains of false beliefs and ideals' (Dewey 1966, 92). Using 'democracy' as a term of convenience, Dewey invites us to see democratic modernisers as political educators who want their readers to be attracted to the new set of civic virtues promoted by the progressive enlightenment. The field of 'intellectual history' reveals that 'the great heroes' are not the many protectors of customary authority but those few thinkers, like Francis Bacon and John Locke, who have promoted the modernising enterprise of intelligence (Dewey 1966, 61–68, 216–218, 281–283). Progressive writers used their communicative power to set up or indeed establish 'a certain kind of inclination and desire' as the norm for a progressive civic culture (Dewey 1966, 357; Fott 2011).

Dewey is very much aware of the wide range of competing virtues circulated in intellectual debates among progressive theorists examined in *Reconstruction in Philosophy* (Dewey 1950). Dewey's interest in pedagogy allows him to bring these variations together as the debatable core sparking the progress towards the distinctive culture or regime of liberal democracy which has become such a widespread model of practical politics. The most influential advocates of progressive modernisation are those writers whose orientation to public discussion took the form of 'a shaking up, a stirring' or 'loosening' of conventional wisdom through what Dewey aptly calls, with echoes of Francis Bacon, 'the invention of inventions' (Dewey 1950, 15–16, 22). The theme of *performance* emerges when Dewey explains that, following the model of Bacon, the greatest progressive writers 'performed an office' of discovery through which they developed, formed and produced 'the intellectual instrumentalities' for what Dewey calls 'secularization', here understood as the 'construction of a moral human science' (Dewey 1950, 25; Horwitz 1987).

Constructions require not only a chief or leading constructor or architect but also implementers, builders and conservers. Bacon is Dewey's exemplar of the progressive enlightener whose architect-like writings reflect a pedagogy of 'philosophical reconstruction'—recharting political communities from ancient to modern sources, with plenty of work left for his reading communities to complete (Dewey 1950, 46–61). Bacon promotes the advancement of learning through his anticipation of 'a certain kind of intelligently conducted doing', later celebrated as the 'operative and experimental' methodology. Bacon's performance overturns classical models of passive contemplation and resembles 'that of the artist producing the painting': here again we note Dewey's theme of the performance of the progressive public intellectual who turns readers away from past forms of spectatorship into modernising forms of experimentation (Dewey 1950, 106; White 1958; Masters and Uhr 2017).

Many of the specifics of Dewey's pedagogy are laid out in his 1910 book *How We Think* (Dewey 1997). The 'pedagogic maxim' guides the learner to approach the abstract through the concrete (Dewey 1997, 139). One important test case relates to 'communication of information', where exercises in communication 'should be supplied by way of stimulus, not with dogmatic finality and rigidity'. The more the communication stimulates 'any process of reflection', the more effective it will be; the model of an effective teacher is an artist capable of fostering 'the attitude of the artist' among followers (Dewey 1997, 197–200, 220–221). Dewey distinguishes between the shallow world of 'instructors' and deeper world of 'teachers'. In his view: 'Genuine communication involves contagion' or something like an influence or eruption, which is one useful way of appreciating the pedagogy of public intellectuals (Dewey 1997, 224). I suggest that our sample of significant political theorists were 'teachers' rather than simply 'instructors'.

The larger sweep of Dewey's picture of Baconian thinkers can be seen in *The Public and Its Problems* originally written in 1927 as a critique of concepts of 'pluralism' (Dewey 1954). Dewey evaluates the plight of liberal democracies as overly pluralised with 'a public too diffused and scattered and too intricate in composition' (Dewey 1954, 137). The so-called 'great society' is a *disintegrated* polity where 'the Public will remain in eclipse' (Dewey 1954, 142). The solution is the transformation of such polities into 'a great community' which will only come about through 'communication' to promote 'shared experience'. Dewey devotes considerable space to examining effective communication: 'dissemination' requires that whatever is distributed so 'as to take root', just as democracy developed over earlier centuries through the careful 'formation of public opinion' (Dewey 1954, 176–177). What Dewey calls 'genuinely public policy' rests on the judgment and estimate of the public (Dewey 1954, 178–179). So too 'genuine social science' rests on the cultivation of 'public judgments' shaped through 'the office of directing opinion'—by public intellectuals inspired by Dewey to exercise leadership 'in the management of publicity' (Dewey 1954, 180–181).

A few intellectuals might obtain such public judgment through a 'secluded library' but the rest of the community requires the arts of presentation in 'the prevalent culture' to carry the message to them. Dewey notes 'the freeing of the artist in literary presentation'—through poetry, drama, the novel—as necessary to bring this type of 'full and moving communication' to fruition (Dewey 1954, 182–184, 197). In the final chapter in *The Public and Its Problems* exploring 'the problem of method', Dewey reflects on his own method as one of the 'expert intellectuals' and member of the 'intellectual aristocracy' to write in ways that 'shape the disposition and beliefs' of citizens (Dewey 1954, 200, 204, 205). Using Tocqueville as one of his examples, Dewey notes how rare it is for 'high-brows' to manage the process of 'discussion and publicity' to promote public persuasion.

The general model of academic criticism used by Dewey is explained in the chapter on the philosophy of language in *Experience and Nature* (Dewey 1958, 166–207). The language of written works of philosophy build bridges between writers and their readers who form communities of discourse, with writers taking influential roles in the two tasks of learning and teaching. Great writers not only display their own learning but also promote the public cultivation of learning through the often-unnoticed teaching roles adopted by progressive public intellectuals when writing works for public consumption. Aware that philosophers 'have discoursed little about discourse itself', Dewy anticipates later intellectual treatments of the role of writers as designers or crafters of community discourse through their calculated use of 'language, the tool of tools' (Dewey 1958, 166–168, 186). Their crafted public language is a product of the 'office of signs' cultivated by progressive intellects as they establish ways their written works can create 'reflection, foresight and recollection' as they 'bridge' the interrelated worlds of writers and readers, or speakers and hearers. A masterful writer 'dramatically identifies himself with potential acts and deeds; he plays many roles…in a contemporaneously enacted drama' (Dewey 1958, 169–170, 185). The task for critics is to recognise that written works contain 'friendly intent' productive of 'communicable meaning' which can instruct readers with the confidence that they are ready now for 'reading the message of things', as is fitting for the progressive enlightenment (Dewey 1958, 174, 181). The role of critics is to 'perceive', to cultivate a 'predictive expectancy' or 'wariness' about the intended consequences likely to be taught to those who begin to understand a truly great work of philosophy (Dewey 1958, 182). In Dewey's terminology, written communication can be 'consummatory as well as instrumental': written works can thus be 'a means of establishing cooperation, domination and order'. Influential great works of philosophy or literature 'supply the meanings in terms of which life is judged, esteemed, and criticized' (Dewey 1958, 202, 204).

Writing as Theorising

I see political theory as one important mode of political activity. I concede that theorists can engage in many types of politics: some progressive, some conservative, with many conventionally liberal in the period of modern political history we are covering. To see political theorists as performing politically means that we are recognising their writing as a form of politics. Dewey provides a solid platform for viewing political theorists as political writers: telling us the story as seen from the safe ground of modern progressivism. A more recent exposition of this view comes from another political philosopher whose work has enriched the academic teaching of the history of modern political thought: the French left-wing academic Claude Lefort (1924–2010). Some of his views about Machiavelli's political theory will emerge later in the chapter on Machiavelli's *The Prince*, reflecting the very useful ways that Lefort's postmodern engagement with Machiavelli can help students appreciate the political dynamism of that revolutionary writer.

Here, however, a more general point about the nature of written political theory can be drawn from Lefort's collection of commentaries on the political enterprise of political philosophy published in English as *Writing: The Political Test* (Lefort 2000). The notion of 'a political test' captures Lefort's thesis that much of the very best political theorising is itself 'a political test' posed by writers for their readers. In a certain sense, Lefort introduces his own tests about politics as he interprets near contemporary writers like Orwell or Rushdie. But more systematically, Lefort uncovers and examines political tests devised by many of the past grand masters of political theory, such as Machiavelli and Tocqueville. These tests emerge as challenges posed by many of these writers in their texts which we tend to treat as high theory and therefore as unlikely to help readers think and act politically. For many of us as readers, our working assumption is that political theory is not really about the practice of politics but is about 'ideologies', taken as the object about which political theorists theorise. Accordingly, a history of modern political theory should move as smoothly as it can on from the slow reading of difficult texts to the faster comprehension of the core sets of 'ideologies' we might expect to see driving this parade of fancy texts. In this way, teachers of Machiavelli tease out of *The Prince* those extracts pertaining to 'Machiavellianism'; teachers of Mill slip through *On Liberty* to reveal the doctrine of 'liberalism' we think Mill used to hold together his somewhat rambling reflections; and teachers of Nietzsche pick and plunder those parts of *On the Genealogy of Morals* thought to reveal the deeper secret of this baffling writer's 'Nietzscheanism'. Interpreters of political theory then proceed to compare these 'systems of ideas' in their de-textualised and therefore somewhat abstract form.

Lefort's interpretation insists that we see the classic texts of modern political theory as more politically complex. His book called *Writing* illustrates how one very able postmodern academic teacher reads those texts: *Writing* is a very significant case study in the arts of astutely reading political texts. Students cannot be expected to be familiar with Lefort's acknowledgement that his own text is about 'a specific mode of writing' associated with 'a certain mode of knowing' (Lefort 2000, xxxix). Surprisingly, he begins his encounter with his examination of what he terms 'literary works': those British works of Orwell and Rushdie. He suggests that such literary works help reveal 'the tests of the political'—testing us as readers about what the nature of 'the political' might be. Lefort contrasts the conventional approach in the history of ideas with his own approach which resembles the kind of reading performed when we encounter literary works, where reading is very much 'an adventure'. Reading theory texts can also be 'an adventure' once we accept that this adventure 'is always rich in new surprises'. Explicitly examining 'the experience of reading', Lefort notes how our close reading of great writing gives us the ability 'to think what is itself seeking to be thought' (Lefort 2000, xl).

Using the examples of Machiavelli and Rousseau, Lefort clarifies the performance of a thinker as a writer by asking us to note in these two models of political philosophy 'what it was *doing*': that it, what their political theory was doing as it shaped their written works. We hear of 'the mobility' often found in the work of the best minds, and we learn that many of the best minds tried to face 'the risky test' of writing in a specific mode allowing them to 'escape from the grips of ideology'. This risky test is managed by writers who compose their written works 'via a series of zig-zag movements' across their texts, 'via a winding path' designed to side-track 'the stupidity of readers' who will step aside with complaints about the 'theory' or its many 'contradictions'. The great thinker-writer 'sets his readers in motion', knowing that 'for some readers' all this 'very controlled form of writing' will start to make sense for those 'capable of hearing him and of placing him within the horizons of their time' (Lefort 2000, xli).

In a complicated conclusion to his Preface, Lefort cites Nietzsche as one of his authorities. The theme is that a thinker like Nietzsche will write in ways that reveal that thinking politically 'goes beyond the bounds of every doctrine or theory'. The interpretative task for readers is to move their minds along the pathways indicated by the writers whose texts they are reading. The challenge explored by Lefort is that for this and so many other thinker-writers, readers cannot simply seek to understand 'what the writer-thinker meant to say'; readers must go further, in ways Lefort tries to demonstrate in his own text of commentary, so that they 'still hear what made him speak' as a writer-thinker (Lefort 2000, xlii). Adding greatly to the complexity of this conclusion, Lefort notes the importance of Leo Strauss as perhaps the most important recent interpreter of 'the art of writing'. We know that Strauss is often cited as a neoconservative, so it comes as something of a surprise to find the postmodernist Lefort acknowledging and later more comprehensively examining, indeed praising, this art of writing in 'Three Notes on Leo Strauss' (Lefort 2000, 172–206). I will return to this examination of Strauss in the final chapter of this book.

Conclusion

We can end this chapter by returning briefly to Dewey who has a high reputation as a leading public intellectual who articulated a 'pragmatic communitarianism' (Welchman 1997, 182–218), later celebrated as 'the communitarian persuasion' required to defend but also to deepen democracy (Selznick 2002, 13–14, 92–93, 151–152). I acknowledge that my sample of three political theorists might be modernisers but not all of them match Dewey's enthusiasm for communitarianism. If Dewey lamented the power of individualism in modern liberalism, then many of our interesting theorists share some of the intellectual responsibility for elevating individuality into such high political prominence. Yet, they did so by using some of the gifts of pedagogy celebrated by Dewey, convinced that their novel renditions of individuality could re-educate readers away from traditional hierarchies and towards what these writers saw as innovative forms of individual excellence. As readers and critics, we owe them our closet attention.

I have used Dewey as a theorist of modernisation who captures important aspects of the pedagogic mind of modernisers. Dewey is the advocate for people power yet here I have used him to showcase some of the powers of the modernising intellectual elite who devised doctrines to benefit the people. Dewey is not the source academic teachers can easily use to bring to life the fine detail at work in great exercises of textual interpretation. Compared to R. G. Collingwood who appears in my final chapter, Dewey offers no real competition for students wanting to see the hard intellectual work of interpreting at close range great written works of political theory. Yet, there is still something very special which

Dewey brings to my topic: and this is his grasp of the public pedagogy at work when many modernising political theorists used their public power as writers to shape and direct the Enlightenment as an educational enterprise. Dewey's portraits of these Baconian modernisers capture the general sense that here we see gifted thinkers acting as very capable writers who use their rhetorical power to construct a series of political cultures (one Machiavellian, another Millian, yet another Nietzschean) offering tantalising rewards for readers left unsatisfied by so many traditional systems of government.

As we get ready in the next chapter to explore Shaftesbury's older ideas of 'soliloquy', we can reflect on Dewey's belief that communication occurs through 'dialogue' involving 'direct give and take'. Less perfect than dialogue is 'soliloquy' where ideas 'are not communicated, shared and reborn' as they can be through dialogue. Soliloquy gives rise to 'broken' thought because the thought is not fully tested through dialogue (Dewey 1954, 218). Soliloquy can reflect wider social communication but it is not the standard way that 'mind emerges'—so often developed through our social speech, including the social art of reading challenging texts, when a person 'dramatically identifies himself with potential acts and deeds; he plays many roles...in a contemporaneously drama'. The warning stated by Dewey is that ancient social thinking worked wonderfully through 'the model of dialectic', and that modern social thinking, in bold experiments of risk-taking, 'composed nature after the model of personal soliloquizing' (Dewey 1958, 170, 173). Was Shaftesbury aware of this potential limitation of 'soliloquy' or was he just another modernising pace-setter showing writers and readers clever ways of self-assurance? The following chapter is my answer.

REFERENCES

Dewey, John. 1950 (1920). *Reconstruction in Philosophy*. New York: Mentor Books.
Dewey, John. 1954 (1927). *The Public and Its Problems*. Athens: Swallow Press/Ohio University Press.
Dewey, John. 1958 (1929). *Experience and Nature*. New York: Dover Publications.
Dewey, John. 1966 (1916). *Democracy and Education*. New York: The Free Press.
Dewey, John. 1997 (1910). *How We Think*. Mineola, NY: Dover Publications.

Fott, David. 2009. John Dewey and the Mutual Influence of Democracy and Education. *The Review of Politics* 71 (1): 7–19.
Fott, David. 2011. John Dewey: Philosophy as Theory of Education. In *Political Philosophy in the Twentieth Century: Authors and Arguments*, ed. Catherine H. Zuckert, 19–31. Cambridge: Cambridge University Press.
Horwitz, Robert. 1987. John Dewey. In *History of Political Philosophy*, 3rd ed., ed. Leo Strauss and Joseph Cropsey, 851–869. Chicago: University of Chicago Press.
Lefort, Claude. 2000. *Writing: The Political Test*, trans. and ed. David Ames Curtis. Durham: Duke University Press.
Masters, Adam, and John Uhr. 2017. *Leadership Performance and Rhetoric*. London: Palgrave.
Selznick, Philip. 2002. *The Communitarian Persuasion*. Washington, DC: Woodrow Wilson Center Press.
Stuhr, John J. 1998. Dewey's Social and Political Philosophy, Chap. 5. In *Reading Dewey: Interpretations for a Postmodern Generation*, ed. Larry A. Rickman, 82–99. Bloomington: Indiana University Press.
Welchman, Jennifer. 1997. *Dewey's Ethical Thought*. Ithaca: Cornell University Press.
White, Howard B. 1958. The Political Faith of John Dewey. *The Journal of Politics* 20 (2): 353–367.

CHAPTER 3

Reading Shaftesbury

Performing as a Critic

Abstract The second lesson comes from Lord Shaftesbury who was tutored by the great theorist John Locke. Shaftesbury developed concepts of criticism and performance as a new way of building bridges between great writers and new readers. Shaftesbury models the way every contemporary academic should perform by teaching the arts of criticism for student-readers to use when engaging with the texts of great writers of political theory.

Keywords Shaftesbury · Criticism · Performance · Writing · Reading Civic virtue

This chapter recovers a view of 'criticism' from one of the founders of the modern role of 'the critic': Anthony Ashley Cooper, also known in his mature life as Lord Shaftesbury (1671–1713). For our purposes, Shaftesbury's concepts of the critic and of criticism articulate the world of performance we (or at least our best writers) can expect of readers. Shaftesbury was, of course, a noted writer and an experienced political figure in British parliamentary politics. The noted British philosopher Gilbert Ryle argued that novelist Jane Austen came from a moral culture

---

The original version of this chapter was revised: Belated author correction has been corrected. The erratum to this chapter is available at https://doi.org/10.1007/978-981-10-7998-6_8

© The Author(s) 2018
J. Uhr, *Performing Political Theory*,
https://doi.org/10.1007/978-981-10-7998-6_3

33

'akin to that of Lord Shaftesbury': her moral ideas 'derived, directly or indirectly, knowingly or unknowingly, from Shaftesbury' (Ryle 1971, 180). This chapter reviews only one part of his many contributions to intellectual history which is his clarification of the type of performance writers expected of their best readers. Being a writer, Shaftesbury knew much about the types of performance favoured by writers, especially those writers seeking to make their mark in promoting modernity while retaining a commitment to classical virtues of humanity—virtues intended to cultivate schemes of individual and civic excellence and to modify what we now term the Lockean 'possessive individualism' mobilised by promoters of liberalism (Carey 2006).

Shaftesbury is not widely known within contemporary political science. His famous private letters to friends revealing his thoughts about the weaknesses in the reigning political doctrine of John Locke are startling in their picture of the spirit of Thomas Hobbes guiding and shaping the hand of Locke (Shaftesbury 1716). But the public figure remains remote. He stands in the background to the study of more prominent figures, often as a representative of enigmatic interests kept in reserve from the major interests dominating history and politics. The Cambridge University Press edition of his masterwork *Characteristics* is a core text in the series devoted to the history of philosophy, edited by an historian of ideas (Shaftesbury 1999). Politics, however, is as important as philosophy or history. Thus it is no surprise that Shaftesbury is visible in studies by political scientists who, for example, study Lockean liberalism (see e.g. Aronson 1959), statesmanship (see e.g. Mansfield 1965, 80, 251 note 22, 252 note 40), Montesquieu (see e.g. Pangle 1973, 222–223, 318, note 28, 323, notes 14 and 16), Hume (see e.g. Danford 1990, 6–7) and, most importantly, 'the lost history of esoteric writing' (see e.g. Melzler 2014, 127–128, 161, 163, 198). From a different perspective, we should also note the quite recent European research publications drawing new attention to Shaftesbury's role in European intellectual history (see e.g. Jaffro 2008, 2014).

Critical Performances

Shaftesbury also knew about the performance of readers, which makes him a useful guide when thinking about the types of performance academic teachers might expect of students reading great works of modern political theory. My view is that Shaftesbury's concept of 'the critic' helps us see and anticipate the type of teaching performed by contemporary academic lecturers whose 'criticism' is one of the core elements in the bridge-building teachers perform when bringing students into the company of great writers. Shaftesbury understood that his scheme of 'criticism' was not really his own 'theory' about literature but was rather his own interpretation of how intermediates (or bridge-builders) between writers and readers could construct what later scholars have confusing termed the 'interactivity' or 'performativity' involved when written texts take on meanings for later audiences. Speaking for audiences who need to know more about virtues of humanity, Shaftesbury is the rare intellectual who also speaks to writers who need to know more about cultivating critics and promoting criticism (Brett 1951; Klein 1994).

The implication for us today is that Shaftesbury models the performance writers might reasonably expect of their most capable readers, and that he models the type of performance we can expect academic educators can use when teaching students about the interpretation of core texts in modern political theory. For contemporary educators, Shaftesbury holds out the promise of awakening our senses of criticism so that we become 'critics' who contribute to the public 'criticism' of civil society: we stand between writers and readers, advising both of how they can enhance their performances when they appreciate their shared relationship in shaping the culture of civic excellence envisaged by Shaftesbury.

Where does Shaftesbury elaborate on the types of performance he thinks important in the activity of criticism? He explores this in his work *Soliloquy* published first in his *Characteristics* and in his later commentary published as 'Miscellany III', also in the *Characteristics* (Shaftesbury 1999, especially 105–108, 147–148; 397, 408–409; see also Klein 1994, 102–107, 203–210; Carey 2006, 120, 125, 133–134; Jaffro 2014). We can anticipate some of the general implications before we examine *Soliloquy* in greater details. This work is itself a great performance by a politically ambitious writer, using his own rhetorical gifts to highlight the substance of the political philosophy readers have a right to expect of their favourite writers. Shaftesbury performs as an advocate for the type of written performance expected of his preferred school of writers. As an experienced critic, Shaftesbury articulates a doctrine of criticism appropriate not only to written performances but also to reading performances. Shaftesbury constructs a bridge of criticism between writers and readers to facilitate their closer relationship as shapers and supporters in a new civic culture (Griffin 1990; Tierney-Hynes 2005). The earliest mention of performance arises when Shaftesbury examines the performance of music, where the performing artist only wants an opportunity to carry out his art 'in the presence of those who are knowing in his art'. The performer needs not simply any audience but instead 'the critical, the nice ear'. Shaftesbury suggests that his criticism can enliven that attentive ear and thereby sharpen the performance of the musician for whom the written musical script is at best the perfect beginning of a musical performance (Shaftesbury 1999, 105).

This use of a musical example is very relevant. The performance of the musicians is caused by the earlier performance of the composer who presumably knew that 'the work of music' exists only in part when the composition is completed: it will exist in greater part when performed, not simply to the personal delight of the composer, but more publicly at a musical concert. The fact that this is the first of Shaftesbury's many references to a performance suggests to me that he also thinks that other written works might also be completed only in part when their composition is completed. We will soon see that Shaftesbury's own work is curiously incomplete: this incompleteness features as a theme of the commentary he himself makes about *Soliloquy* in 'Miscellany III' (Shaftesbury 1999, 395–399). Just as musical scores require performers and an audience to transform the script into a performance, so too a range of written texts require readers to help generate the performance of attentive interpretation expected of the text by the author. Shaftesbury demonstrates the value of this sort of criticism of his own work when he uses 'Miscellany III' to bring out many obscurities and underdeveloped themes in *Soliloquy*. That is, Shaftesbury when acting in the third 'Miscellany' as critic, sharpens the interpretative attention of readers to the *Soliloquy* written by Shaftesbury as the author of this promising but puzzling text—notably called a 'performance' (Shaftesbury 1999, 147). What works for music works for all the muses. It seems that in 'every science, every art' the authors need their performances searched and examined 'by all the rules of art and nicest criticism' (Shaftesbury 1999, 106). All the performing arts require 'an art of hearing'. What makes for a performance is not only actors of ability but also an audience informed by criticism: hence, performers do what they can by way of 'improving and refining the public ear'. Critics emerge as 'interpreters to the people' who teach the public 'what was just and excellent in each performance' (Shaftesbury 1999, 108). Shaftesbury argues that readers of written texts 'judge of the performance' of those works. This will only occur where critics like Shaftesbury have performed their own magic by giving audiences an education in taste, and giving writers an education in the excellence of the virtues. Those writers who appreciate 'the idea of perfection' can look forward to their work being accepted as a 'performance'—as exemplified by Milton's *Paradise Lost* (Shaftesbury 1999, 160).

From Critic to Criticism

Lord Shaftesbury is the author of *Characteristics* (1711): a long work of nearly 500 pages which includes one particular work of nearly 100 pages which is the *Soliloquy or Advice to an Author* (see e.g. Shaftesbury 1999, 70–162). This neglected work in modern philosophy refers to the role of 'performance' and 'performers' many times, as Shaftesbury clarifies the roles of great authors as clever artists. Yet Shaftesbury is largely neglected in the standard field of the history of political thought (see however: Charles Taylor 1992, 248–259). My case is that Shaftesbury is one of the few theorists who has examined the art of writing as a cultural practice: informing and shaping the public culture, often through a rhetoric of innovation. As a close colleague of his tutor and mentor John Locke—who had been a close colleague of the first Lord Shaftesbury during the 1688 Revolution (see e.g. Ryan 2012, 454–455, 513)—Shaftesbury appreciated that readers had to become 'critics' to interpret the publications of great thinkers who often disguised key concepts in deceptive prose. For us, Shaftesbury is useful as 'a bridge' between writers and readers: he is a thinker of real importance who had considerable experience as a politician, serving in the House of Commons from 1695 and the House of Lords from 1700—before dying in Italy in 1713 at the young age of 42.

His *Soliloquy* builds the 'bridge' we speak of, helping readers learn the arts of 'criticism' so that they can critically engage with thinkers, like Locke, for example, who are convinced that many of their most important political thoughts should be published not directly but obliquely—for fear of being misunderstood by their friends as well as their opponents. Klein notes that, compared to many thinkers of the Enlightenment, Shaftesbury is more 'optimistic' and has greater 'confidence in human sociability', consistent with his project of 'educating humanity' (Klein 1999, vii). Part of this education involves turning able readers into effective 'critics' who can move across the 'bridge' between theory and practice. Shaftesbury was one of the first promoters of 'civilization' where that historical process develops a literate 'sensibility'—reflecting the agenda of 'politeness' which found expression not only in personal conduct but also in published thoughts and expressions. A 'polite' theorist of politics might arrange their published thoughts in ways that would not 'politicise'—but might, to adapt a key Shaftesbury term, 'publicise'—civil society. As a theorist of the *sensus communis*, Shaftesbury promoted philosophical writing likely to encourage the moral sensibility of 'politeness' which has been accepted an important early *communitarian* contribution to modern liberalism—most evident in his careful analysis of 'the dynamics and politics of culture' (Klein 1999, xii).

This is not the place to spell out all of the details contained in Shaftesbury's *Soliloquy* with its unusual examination of 'the roles of the social and political elite, of critics, and…the people' (Klein 1999, xii). A 'polite' author practices a rhetoric which contributes to civil liberties by weakening or minimising conventional rhetorics described by Shaftesbury as 'magisterial' or authoritarian. Liberal scepticism appears as an attribute of Shaftesbury, although scholars debate extensively whether this prince of critics tried to moderate public morality because of a commitment to modern liberalism or alternatively a commitment to premodern or 'Socratic' liberalism (Aronson 1959; Grean 1967, 15–18). In works like *Soliloquy*, Shaftesbury drew on both sources of liberalism 'to make philosophers of readers' (Klein 1999, xiv). This type of 'criticism' allowed Shaftesbury to highlight some of the pathways we follow in the later chapters of this book. Of these pathways, one of the most prominent is 'enchantment' which is the term used by Shaftesbury to identify the role of literary rhetoric so often encountered when reading demanding works of political theory. Great writers become great not simply because they can move our intellects but also because they use 'the power of moving the affections' through enchantment (Shaftesbury 1999, 107). Great writers can be 'enchanters', sometimes lulling ordinary readers into peace and security through well-intentioned fables, and at other times arousing extraordinary readers with promising suggestions of philosophy for those prepared to follow the hazardous pathway (Brett 1951, 100–108, 128–130; Jaffro 2014).

Soliloquy reveals how thinkers who want to be writers have to establish a 'dialogue' with readers; this work also reveals how readers who want to understand great writers have to anticipate their role in this 'dialogue' as co-respondents following the writer's 'own meaning and design' (Shaftesbury 1999, 84). Following Shaftesbury, we help where we can to construct this effective 'bridge' between writers and readers which remains elusive for so many contemporary students of the history of political theory. Our inspiration to think through as Shaftesbury urges us to do helps us help our students: following Shaftesbury, we can identify the theorist who can move us as an exemplary *virtuoso* whose writings can be distinguished from 'the profound researches of pedants' who tend to dominate the world of scholarship (Shaftesbury 1999, 148–149). In later chapters, this book examines three of the leading *virtuosi* who make the grade as great authors worthy of Shaftesbury's respect.

The Nature of the Critic

Shaftesbury's text is a work of 'advice to an author'. Shaftesbury is the author of this advice but he is not the author for whom this advice has been prepared. His *Soliloquy* is the first term used in this advice, as though the receiver of the advice should see his writing role in terms of a soliloquy—where one speaks alone, out of reach of or unaware of any listeners. He refers to the concept of 'soliloquy' frequently in this work, partly because he thinks that writers need to hear what he has to say about the benefits of 'soliloquy' and partly because he himself is engaged in a 'soliloquy': the defender of reading is ruminating with his other self who is, of course, a writer. The core contention is that writers need to use 'soliloquy' to 'play the critic' on themselves. Writers have two competing tendencies: they can be either *inward*—when they write to satisfy their personal interests—or they can be *outward*—when they write to satisfy their public interests. Shaftesbury warns writers that their outward tendencies enslave them to the power of 'fancy' as they compose works intended to please the indulgent opinion of the widest range of public readers they can enlist. The warning is that writers should look inward, listen to the advice that comes from their heart, so that they can write in what we might term 'fancy-free' ways independent of the flimsy opinion of their audience (Griffin 1990; Tierney-Hynes 2005).

Modelling his advice, Shaftesbury engages in a public dialogue with himself, using his own 'soliloquy' to dramatise the power of what he carefully calls this 'method' of criticism (see e.g. Shaftesbury 1999, 79, 84, 115–116, 131, 137, 139, 146–147, 162). In fact, Shaftesbury compounds his dramatic engagement by supplementing his lengthy text with a set of 'miscellaneous reflections', including 'Miscellany III' which reads as though it were another writer's commentary or dialogue on Shaftesbury's *Soliloquy* (Shaftesbury 1999, 395–418). Thus the text as written by Shaftesbury contains two works in the *Characteristics*: the third 'treatise' plus the third 'Miscellany'. These two works tease out the writer's inward dialogue between the two sides of his character—with readers learning to see how his 'will' moderates the competing energies of the two selves within: noble but often weak *reason* and the often inordinate lesser capacity of *passion*.

Shaftesbury is not engaged in autobiography. He is using himself as an example so that readers can understand how his 'advice to an author' might work. Clearly, the writer Shaftesbury knows that his readers include people who are not writers. He is writing advice to authors through the medium of writing to readers. He writes as though he wants authors to know what their readers now expect of them; but he is also writing to readers about what to expect of authors, of whom he represents a distinct type interested in new forms of contribution by 'critics' to 'criticism'. The mode of presentation makes it hard for readers quickly to seize on the core concepts of Shaftesbury's argument: the *Soliloquy* has three parts, each of which contains three sections; and the third 'Miscellany' has two chapters. This complicated architecture encourages many of Shaftesbury's academic commentators to be very selective in what they identify as his core themes or core arguments, with the result that there is a wide variation in the Shaftesbury scholarship.

More still needs to be done to recover Shaftesbury's own understanding of relationships within his fragmented writings. Here we can make our own contribution by examining more closely his ideas on the critic as the bridge-builder between writers and readers and criticism as the interpretative art writers should expect of their best readers. The critic is the author of the *Soliloquy* writ large; criticism is the body of argument contained in the 'advice' presented in the *Soliloquy* (Voitle 1984, 333–338; Griffin 1990; Tierney-Hynes 2005; Jaffro 2008, 263–267).

We can begin by tracing the movement of argument in section one of Part One (Shaftesbury 1999, 70–76). The *Soliloquy* invites readers to learn 'the rules of criticism' so that they can begin 'to play the critic'. Shaftesbury begins by reporting 'the dangerous part of advising', noting how many authors engage as advisors 'secretly', almost hiding 'the way and manner of advising'. The *Soliloquy* could be true to this advertised form of indirect advising: that is, the practice of a soliloquy might not really be what Shaftesbury is advising authors to adopt. If this is correct, then we can see that Shaftesbury is using the example of a soliloquy to advise authors on more systematic rethinking of relationships between authors and audiences. The practice of a soliloquy is a useful preamble to the longer journey of this rethinking about the vices of corruption and the virtues of integrity in writing. The many examples of effective soliloquy described by Shaftesbury highlight the corrupt power of 'fancy' or 'opinion' in relationships between authors and audiences. These soliloquies illustrate the beginnings of a recovery by authors of their 'true selves' or their 'inner selves' as they wash out the corrosive force of fanciful relationships driven by the self-interest of conventional audiences preferring to be entertained but not really instructed. In this way, a soliloquy is an 'anticipating remedy' or a 'method of evacuation' from the ills of the 'froth and scum' of the author–audience relationship—which is governed by 'the exuberance of conceit and fancy'. The defect of corruption facing authors comes from the 'mighty heat and ebullition of fancy'; the overcoming of this defect comes from the practice of soliloquy which teach authors how 'to play the critic thoroughly upon himself'.

Section two reveals more about the positive learning which should come on the heels of the negative 'self-discoursing practice' of soliloquy (Shaftesbury 1999, 76–85). Soliloquy works its magic by giving authors an opportunity to 'know themselves'; it works because it provides authors with 'a kind of vocal looking glass' allowing authors to recognise their two selves—including that unreasonable self (that is, 'appetite') which tends to pursue a 'courtship to the public' which 'takes him out of himself', devoted to this 'mistress' whose 'grace and favour he solicits'. The other or more reasonable self ('reason') turns in another direction, modelled by the 'self-entertainment' of 'the man of sense, the sage or philosopher'. Shaftesbury now speaks of 'two distinct separate souls' when examining 'two persons in one individual self'. The leading edge is the less reasonable self often dependent on 'humour and fancy' or 'fancy and opinion'—by which Shaftesbury means the opinionated fancy many readers use to render potentially independent authors corruptly dependent. This occurs where there is 'no certain inspector or auditor' to restrain the power of corrupt influence, with Shaftesbury using the image of soliloquy to reflect the counter-power of 'a real pedagogue' able to overrule the 'persecution' exercised by audiences over authors. The work sketches a moral psychology with 'will' struggling between the conflicting demands of reason and appetite, with authors using 'inward rhetoric' to manage will and overcome its alternative power 'to speak by nods and winks' and so act like 'mere sophisters and imposters'.

Section three concludes the first part with an account of 'a liberal education' to liberate authors from corrupt dependency (Shaftesbury 1999, 85–94). Here Shaftesbury uses 'the Socratic texts' as models of proper authorship, working their own magic by acting as 'a looking-glass' or even 'a sort of pocket-mirror' so that readers can be taught 'to know ourselves'. The implication is that authors can recover this mode of writing of 'well-practised dialogists' who teach readers about the larger set of virtues and vices minimised in their own self-centred struggles between reason and appetite. Shaftesbury compares 'this mirror writing' with conventional modern types of 'more complaisant, modish' writing which force the modern author to match their work 'to the fancy of his reader' whom he 'constantly caresses and cajoles'. The 'ancient manner of writing' differed because it was generally impersonal, with silent or invisible or indirect authors (quite like their imitator Shaftesbury) using their skill to teach readers about virtues and vices.

The three sections of part two examine the specific 'influences' of three types of audience capable of shaping the way authors write: those 'in power', the critics and the people. The critics appear between the rulers and the ruled, possibly capable of regulating aspects of both the rulers and the ruled. Shaftesbury argues that both rulers and the ruled corrupt writers by making them unduly dependent on either the high power of 'the great' or the surprisingly strong public power of key audiences. By contrast, critics have the potential to promote the integrity of writers by defending their independence.

Section one deals with 'the enchantment' which rulers have held over writers, especially poets who traditionally have spun tales to celebrate 'the great' or at least those who want to be thought 'great' who have the power to rob writers of their genuine independence. Shaftesbury mentions 'princes', 'nobles', 'potentates', 'grandees' and 'prime ministers' who exercise great power generally on their own terms, with 'the least care or culture' from the best advisers in the intellectual world of arts and sciences. Compared to foreign nations, Britain suffers little from 'the disorders and misery of the great'; but for how long can its people rest assured that whoever advises the great and those who want to be great 'to idolize the next in power above them and think nothing so adorable as that unlimited greatness and tyrannic power' wielded by those who rule? Can 'virtue and emulation' break the potential power of vice and tyranny? Shaftesbury warns rulers that 'their fame is in the hands of penmen' who can, in turn, be excelled or ruined by the powerful.

The nation needs 'worthy poetic geniuses' and 'able penmen'; so too, statesmen—'our Alexanders'—need 'the signal poet or herald of fame'. Shaftesbury steadily advances his claim that as a new prince of poetry, inspired as we shall see by Aristotle's *Poetics*, he can promote or at least initiate a new culture of liberal learning. Noting that Britain is a polity where 'the people are sharers in power', Shaftesbury calls on government to promote the arts and sciences: in part to restrain the public from improperly favouring 'pretenders'; and in part to strengthen the public's better instinct to support primarily those writers and artists with deserving 'merit' (Shaftesbury 1999, 94–103).

Section two is very near the centre of the *Soliloquy* so it is no surprise that it deals with the central role of critics who appear to writers as either 'the enchanters' talking up their work or 'the persecutors' condemning their work (Shaftesbury 1999, 103–117). The challenge for Shaftesbury is to clarify the valuable role of critics as defenders of the integrity of writers. Criticism is the art of critics, now examined as a form of rhetoric because of its very close understanding of the power of persuasion. For 'chief men and leaders', persuasion is reduced to 'the craft of pleasing': hence, 'to charm the public ear and to incline the heart by the agreeableness of expression' is the task performed by those aiming for public power, who appreciate that 'the people have to be convinced before they acted'. Criticism arises from 'the persuasive arts' but it competes with rival 'enchanting arts' in striving to cultivate 'the public ear'. The first critics were 'sophists' by which Shaftesbury means that these first critics defended public space against the intrusion of enchanters' 'specious and pretending' private speech: defending 'the common ear' against the 'affected graces of mere pretenders'. Shaftesbury identifies Aristotle as 'the prince of critics' and contends that his *Poetics* is the standard for the art of criticism. Aristotle is 'the first who gained repute in the methodic kind', based on his *Poetics* and his companion *Rhetoric* and their related accounts of the two worlds of persuasion—the sublime and the comic— and their related 'way of form and method' known as 'the didactive or perceptive'. Modern authors have lost or forgotten these methods, especially the use of the comic 'method of exposing folly, pedantry, false reason and ill writing'.

Section three examines how writers relate to the public, which allows Shaftesbury to show that the dynamic relationship is really between the demanding public and compliant writers (Shaftesbury 1999, 117–125). Here we see a comparison between those greater artists who treasure 'the justness and truth of work' and those lesser artists who fail to retain honest rules of art, preferring instead to flatter the 'first relish and appetite' of their audience. The focus now is 'virtue, real virtue' as a quality that is 'independent of opinion'. The most gifted writers 'had not always the world on their side'. They wrote independently but with the hope of attracting readers and listeners: initially ignored by the world, they 'forced their way into it'. Thus the greatest writers 'formed their audience, polished the age, refined the public ear and framed it right'. By contrast, many 'modern authors' act differently because they 'accommodate themselves to the genius of the age': in his own times, Shaftesbury declares that 'the audience makes the poet'—whereas in classical times, the poet made the audience. Curiously for us, Shaftesbury uses humour as his standard, implying that writers who help readers laugh at vice do more to promote virtue than many modern writers who tend to have 'a killing disposition' used to make readers laugh at pretended virtue which is revealed as hidden vice. He uses Shakespeare as a model of a writer capable of using humour to help audiences better understand the unconventional deeper nature of human virtue and the threats which vice can bring to those uncommitted to virtue as a form of human excellence. He also uses the poet Milton as another English example of writing excellence, arguing that he and Shakespeare 'command their audience and establish a good taste' as their contribution to building or shaping a community. These examples prove Shaftesbury's point that effective writers 'must borrow of the philosopher' and use their works to cultivate virtue in both its human and civic qualities.

Section one of Part Three ascends abruptly into elevated analysis of moral psychology as Shaftesbury examines 'the regulation and government' of the human passions associated with virtuous character (Shaftesbury 1999, 125–135). The passions of 'anger, ambition, love, desire' and so on frame what we come to think of as our 'interests'. The problem is that not all of our passionate 'interests' measure up as worthy of what should indeed be our '*scope* and *end*' as excellent human beings. The theme here is to relate the passions which move us in one direction or another to what we might see as their drivers, one of which is singled out for very close examination: 'opinion' or vulgar reputation which often has great power as an 'imposture' and sometimes even an enemy of virtue. Philosophy emerges as the 'excellent mistress' to rival that unreliable mistress of 'opinion', and as the source of that intellectual discipline capable of 'teaching me to know myself'. In this section, Shaftesbury raises up readers' hopes of 'the philosophical art' but only by comparing his many important questions about the nature of human virtue with the unpromising modern philosophies which seem sceptical, to say the very least, of virtue as a natural category of human nature.

Section two ascends even further into philosophy as Shaftesbury adopts the method of a devil's advocate by making a case against the kind of moral philosophy he seems to be searching for, with his imaginary dialogue about the power of 'fancy' to establish whatever 'interests' the fanciful might want to pursue (Shaftesbury 1999, 136–147). Could it really be that our selfish interests in pleasure determine whatever we take to be good? Shaftesbury lets his imagined reader wonder about this complaint against the missing philosophy of virtue. This section documents in vivid detail the characteristics of 'the side of corrupt interest and a wrong self'. The purpose seems to be to let readers recognise the widely acknowledged claims but more importantly the rarely accepted limits of what Shaftesbury calls 'pleasure merely'. Imagining a gallery of fancies hard at work to lure us away from virtue, Shaftesbury nudges his readers to wonder what type of 'controller or manager' can contend against this gravest threat to philosophy, which is the doctrine promoted by the fancies: 'Everything is right, if anything be so, because I fancy it'. The section sketches a struggle between reason and passion in a bold literary way, as though Shaftesbury was writing a novel rather than reflecting on philosophy. It seems that he is doing both: this section suggests that the best type of philosophy of human virtue will come from 'the skill and art of a good writer' who can reduce vice and elevate virtue by making us 'wittier and politer'. Shaftesbury's sketch reads like a novella as it dramatises the 'method of inward colloquy' urged on good writers.

The final third section is almost twice as long as earlier sections but again there is little substantive philosophy; what dominates this section is Shaftesbury's ridicule of conventional scholarship as anti-philosophical (Shaftesbury 1999, 147–162). The section has more lively writing than many earlier sections, with Shaftesbury practising his own writing skills with his character assassination of those scholars who write and display their 'sophistry and pedantic learning'. While philosophy remains an unseen art, its practitioners are very much in sight: the unconventional 'virtuosos' who are more likely to be greater writers than the conventional scholars because they have that 'right taste' which Shaftesbury calls 'civility and humanity'. The writing of scholars will reflect 'the profound researches of pedants' who know so little about what philosophy knows so much: virtue as human excellence. Some scholars might seem to write well if they resemble 'a mock-virtuoso or mere pedant', but their work will or should attract only a small audience because they have 'no ear or eye' for the admirable virtues or indeed the alluring vices. Readers learn that 'formalists of this sort' know what they know but not what readers really want to know which is the strength of virtue and the weakness of vice. Compared to 'the virtuoso tribe', these scholarly writers seem ridiculous because they write formally rather than as artists. Shaftesbury defines the 'the writing artist' as the one who can 'represent merit and virtue or mark deformity and blemish' and he then refines his definition with his challenging contention that 'mere lies, judiciously composed, can teach us the truth of things beyond any other manner'. Politely acknowledging the contribution that sacred literature can make to worthy writing, Shaftesbury concludes this section and indeed the *Soliloquy* as a whole by gently advising, in this work of advice, that 'honest home-philosophy' can teach us how best to know ourselves.

The Style of Writing

One productive way of bringing Shaftesbury forward is to note his place in Ginsberg's collection of edited essays on *The Philosopher as Writer* (Ginsberg 1987). This set of essays on eighteenth century philosophy and rhetoric demonstrates the value of examining thinkers as writers. For instance, Ginsberg notes that David Hume chose to write dialogues about natural religion: 'cushioning the reader from the blows of arguments that severed divinity from human knowledge and concealing the author's position amid the interlocutors' (Ginsberg 1987, 7). Hume's essays on such topics as taste were used as 'a literary strategy…to cause the reader to experience what Hume was talking about' (Ginsberg 1987, 10). We also learn that Rousseau devised a rhetoric of discourse when 'trying to persuade the reader of what he cannot demonstrate' (Ginsberg 1987, 9). These and many other eighteenth-century thinkers knew that their ideas were 'susceptible to suppression when expressed straightforwardly' (Ginsberg 1987, 10). This matches Shaftesbury's view that wise writers accepted the necessity 'to speak in parables, and with a double meaning, that the enemy be amused, and they only who have ears to hear may hear' (quoted Grean 1967, 109).

Robert Markley's chapter on 'Style as Philosophical Structure' examines Shaftesbury's *Characteristics* in this rhetorical context (Markley 1987, 140–154). Shaftesbury's style of writing 'puzzled Locke' who was a close friend of the writer, but one who feared that Shaftesbury's work was 'part revelation, part complex game'. Understanding style as 'an affective process', Shaftesbury uses language which 'embodies and deploys a system of values'. At the centre of this system is his 'insistent idealism' reflecting what he takes to be 'perfection', with an 'idealization of the artist' near the peak of this perfectionist ascent. The aim is not to cultivate new artists but to propagate new critics who can bridge and bring together the two worlds of writers and readers, much as Shaftesbury thinks he is doing in what Markley rightly calls his 'performance' of criticism, with its many 'languages of regeneration' to cultivate perfection—or at least excellence—among readers and writers (Markley 1987, 143, 147–148, 153).

CONCLUSION

There are other useful explorations of thinkers as writers. Berel Lang's 'Towards a Poetics of Philosophical Discourse' (Lang 1980a), *Philosophical Style* (Lang 1980b) and *The Anatomy of Philosophical Style* (Lang 1990) are impressive, as is Richetti's *Philosophical Writing* (Richetti 1983). Lang's (1990) book examines 'the politics of interpretation' since at least the time of Spinoza when critics have suspected that this philosopher wrote carefully—to put off enemies but also to attract friends, indirectly. Lang uses Spinoza to support his case against the conventional wisdom of what he calls the 'neutralist' model of interpretation which does what it can to extract 'the structure of philosophical assertion' from the literary texts where they are located. Lang's alternative model emerges from what he sees as 'concealment or repression' which causes thinkers like Spinoza, or more impressively Plato, to hide many of their own thoughts behind the cast of characters who dominate, for example, the Platonic dialogues. Lang's alternative model is one of 'interaction' between form and content, where the style of the written text 'makes the philosopher'. Writers can be seen as 'emplotting' their written works: performing by 'doing and making' something that is very far from being 'a disembodied text' (Lang 1990, 18–23).

For our purposes, the one invaluable source on Shaftesbury is the work on the revival of Platonism in Renaissance England by Ernst Cassirer (Cassirer 1953). The reference to 'Platonism' indicates how Cassirer reads Shaftesbury: as a stylist shaped by the style begun by Plato. Cassirer's important work of historical investigation draws extensively on Shaftesbury's *Soliloquy* as a modern formulation of Platonic criticism, albeit a formulation that is very much a friend of modernity with only limited longing for the philosophy or politics of classical antiquity. Shaftesbury emerges as 'the first great aesthetician that England produced', with his *Soliloquy* promoting a concept of 'taste' that was to prove powerful especially in the development of German theories of the arts. Shaftesbury's private critique of Locke as a disciple of Hobbes makes the public Shaftesbury more remarkable as a scholar tutored by the great Locke yet never wholly under Locke's guidance (Shaftesbury 1716). Shaftesbury's works are credited by Cassirer as the 'creation of genuine and lofty philosophic poetry'. The role of humour in Shaftesbury's thought is recognised as a core part of Shaftesbury's philosophical rhetoric, where 'rhetoric' stands for persuasive writing and not deceptive miswriting (Cassirer 1953, 166–171; see also Critchley 2002, 80–85). Shaftesbury's anxiety over the remarkable power of John Locke's sober rhetoric of a scheme of individualism much indebted to the political theory of Hobbes provoked him to reshape the political culture of modern Britain—a fitting endeavour to one known as 'Europe's amiable Plato' (Cassirer 1953, 189–194, 199).

References

Aronson, Jason. 1959. Critical Note: Shaftesbury on Locke. *American Political Science Review* 53 (4): 1101–1104.
Brett, R.L. 1951. *The Third Earl of Shaftesbury*. London: Hutchinson's University Library.
Carey, Daniel. 2006. *Locke, Shaftesbury and Hutcheson: Contesting Diversity in the Enlightenment and Beyond*. Cambridge: Cambridge University Press.
Cassirer, Ernst. 1953. *The Platonic Renaissance in England*, trans. James P. Pettegrove. London: Nelson.
Critchley, Simon. 2002. *On Humour*. London: Routledge.
Danford, John W. 1990. *David Hume and the Problem of Reason*. New Haven: Yale University Press.
Ginsberg, Robert (ed.). 1987. *The Philosopher as Writer*. London: Associated University Presses.
Grean, Stanley. 1967. *Shaftesbury's Philosophy of Religion and Ethics*. Athens: Ohio University Press.
Griffin, Susan. 1990. Shaftesbury's Soliloquy: The Development of Rhetorical Authority. *Rhetoric Review* 9 (1): 94–106.
Jaffro, Laurent. 2008. Which Platonism for Which Modernity? Chap. 17. In *Platonism at the Origins of Modernity*, ed. Douglas Hedley and Sarah Hutton, 255–267. Dordrecht: Springer.

Jaffro, Laurent. 2014. Cyrus' Strategy: Shaftesbury on Human Frailty and the Will. In *New Ages, New Opinions: Shaftesbury in His World and Today*, ed. Patrick Mueller, 153–165. Frankfurt: Peter Lang.
Klein, Lawrence E. 1994. *Shaftesbury and the Culture of Politeness*. Cambridge: Cambridge University Press.
Klein, Lawrence E. 1999. 'Introduction' to *Shaftesbury's Characteristics*, vii–xxxi. Cambridge: Cambridge University Press.
Lang, Berel. 1980a. Towards a Poetics of Philosophical Discourse. *The Monist* 63 (4): 445–464.
Lang, Berel. 1980b. *Philosophical Style*. Chicago: University of Chicago Press.
Lang, Berel. 1990. *The Anatomy of Philosophical Style*. Oxford: Blackwell.
Mansfield, Harvey J., Jr. 1965. *Statesmanship and Party Government*. Chicago: University of Chicago Press.
Markley, Robert. 1987. Style as Philosophical Structure. In *The Philosopher as Writer*, ed. Robert Ginsberg, 140–154. London: Associated University Presses.
Melzer, Arthur M. 2014. *Philosophy Between the Lines*. Chicago: University of Chicago Press.
Pangle, Thomas L. 1973. *Montesquieu's Philosophy of Liberalism*. Chicago: University of Chicago Press.
Richetti, John T. 1983. *Philosophical Writing: Locke, Berkeley, Hume*. Cambridge, MA: Harvard University Press.
Ryan, Alan. 2012. *On Politics*. London: Penguin Books.
Ryle, Gilbert. 1971. Jane Austen and the Moralists, Chap. 8. In *English Literature and British Philosophy*, ed. S.P. Rosenbaum, 168–183. Chicago: University of Chicago Press.
Shaftesbury, Lord. 1716. *Several Letters Written by a Noble Lord to a Young Man at the University*. London: J. Roberts, available as a e-book through the British Library.
Shaftesbury, Lord. 1999. Soliloquy. In *Characteristics*, ed. L.E. Klein, 70–162. Cambridge: Cambridge University Press.
Taylor, Charles. 1992. *Sources of the Self*. Cambridge: Cambridge University Press.
Tierney-Hynes, Rebecca. 2005. Shaftesbury's Soliloquy: Authorship and the Psychology of Romance. *Eighteenth Century Studies* 38 (4): 605–621.
Voitle, Robert. 1984. *The Third Earl of Shaftesbury*. Baton Rouge: Louisiana State University Press.

CHAPTER 4

Reading Machiavelli's *The Prince*

Performing as a Prince

Abstract The third lesson comes from Machiavelli. *The Prince* is a classic text in modern political theory. This chapter reveals the style of performance carried out by Machiavelli as he wrote *The Prince* to re-educate readers into new ways of thinking and acting politically. Why is this important text so difficult to understand? Because Machiavelli wanted readers to work out many theoretical things for themselves, which is his gift to the teaching of political theory.

Keywords Machiavelli · Virtu · *The Prince* · Innovation · Founders Flexibility

Students of politics are frequently interested in Machiavelli and do not need too much persuading to turn to his exemplary *The Prince* (Machiavelli 1998). Students interested in the academic study of politics quickly (but not always carefully) learn that Machiavelli stands out as 'a realist' whose works like *The Prince* reveal what many regard as hard truths about power politics. Even before they have read a page from *The Prince*, students already know something about 'Machiavellianism': the idea that rulers should 'be prepared to do evil if good will come of

---

The original version of this chapter was revised: Belated author correction has been corrected. The erratum to this chapter is available at
https://doi.org/10.1007/978-981-10-7998-6_8

© The Author(s) 2018
J. Uhr, *Performing Political Theory*,
https://doi.org/10.1007/978-981-10-7998-6_4

51

it' (Skinner 1988, xxiv). This grim doctrine of cynical politics comes in many forms: minimally, it can refer to wily deception to hide individual self-interest; more comprehensively, it can refer to the deceptive use of force and fraud in the hard grind of politics, even as practised by those promoting broadly public rather than narrowly personal interests.

Machiavelli's experience of politics drew on both of these forms of individual and collective interest. Machiavelli exercised considerable public power as a leading city official, a diplomat and as an adviser to the government (Skinner 1981, 3–47). It therefore helps if students are interested in knowing something about the personal political activities of Machiavelli, especially if this relates to his decision to write *The Prince* as an exercise in rehabilitation: winning new favours from former enemies who, to protect the new Medici administration, had forced him out of public office as a prominent city official in Florence (Skinner 1988, ix–x; Viroli 2000, 119–140).

Why Start with Machiavelli?

Sources like De Grazia's *Machiavelli in Hell* provide lecturers with more than enough historical information to guide students to see Machiavelli as a seasoned practitioner as well as a grand theorist of politics. It helps to know what Machiavelli's professional life as a significant public official was like when he was 'on the job' (De Grazia 1996, 16–28). But the most important hint lecturers can give about the strange nature of Machiavelli's 'rehabilitation' with those who forced him out of office is that *The Prince* is much more than a clever job application and much more than a stylish 'mirror of princes' flattering the new regime which ousted the writer Niccolo. *The Prince* is much more about theories and practices of 'the new prince' than the conventional rule of old or even existing princes (Skinner 1988; de Grazia 1996, 232–240). Lecturers can do something important to prepare students in readiness for Machiavelli's extraordinary innovation by alerting them to this theme of 'the new prince' about to be described in what might appear to be a work summarising the conventional wisdom of ruling and being ruled. The formal Latin title of the work reads in English as 'On Principalities'—and not 'On Princes'. Understandably we give the work the title of 'The Prince' because the core theme addressed by Machiavelli is that, wherever possible, the prince should define the nature of the principality: the principality is the medium but the message comes from the prince, especially 'the new prince' who is the subject of Machiavelli's real message in this influential text (Lefort 2000, 109–141).

What does 'newness' here mean? According to critics like de Grazia, it refers 'to a concept somewhat different from common usage', meaning that we focus not simply on those new to the job of ruling principalities but instead on those who arise as 'a heroic figure' worthy of performing 'the heroic role': to use one of Machiavelli's core terms, this new prince is 'extraordinary' as we soon begin to discover as we start to read the 'menacing text of *The Prince*' (De Grazia 1996, 233–239). Students can be encouraged when they learn that the 'new' prince could even be the next new reader of *The Prince*: a text with 'an undercurrent of specific warning' only accessible if readers are taught to search 'beneath the surface generalities' (Skinner 1988, xiii).

Why Start with *The Prince*?

Machiavelli is a classic great thinker whose works typically begin university courses examining the history of modern political thought. As lecturers, we invite students to start with Machiavelli's relatively short *The Prince* because this book helped launch modernity, despite the critical reputation Machiavelli attracts as a symbol of the Renaissance and a reviver of antiquity. The view that 'Machiavelli is the first openly revolutionary political philosopher' credits *The Prince* as a work of very great public propaganda—or 'enlightenment' if that term makes it sound more appealing (Pangle and Burns 2015, 201; Strauss 1984, 62, 232–234, 295–299; Skinner 1981, 31–47; Mansfield 1996, 258–263). There is so much contentious commentary on Machiavelli that our task as lecturers had been to use as little of that commentary as that can help us quickly get the students reading Machiavelli's *The Prince* to work out this great thinker's political theories for themselves, unmediated by remorseless criticism of Machiavelli's personal philosophy or 'Machiavellianism'.

With some risk, however, as lecturers we decided to assemble one short and narrow bridge of potentially helpful commentary between our world as contemporary students of politics and Machiavelli's world captured in *The Prince*. This bridge was constructed around Isaiah Berlin's famous (at least to us as students of Machiavelli) article 'The Question of Machiavelli' which is a useful review of many of the potential interpretations scholars have provided about the core questions posed by this greatly influential thinker at the dawn of modernity (Berlin 1971). Our course would eventually make its way to Berlin's even-more-famous writings on negative and positive liberty written in the late 1950s, where we would invite students to see what non-Machiavellian use Berlin had himself made of core concepts of liberty, and compare how this interpretation works with our own reading of Mill's *On Liberty* which was Berlin's original object of study (Berlin 1969). But that is not the immediate interest here, where our interest is to record how Berlin's 1971 article has proven useful in at least three instructive ways.

First, the Berlin article warns students that there are many schools of thought competing to help us read Machiavelli as a modernist or as a classicist or as a Renaissance figure caught between modernity and antiquity or as an innovative religious enthusiast or as a pioneer Italian patriot or as student of the scientific study of politics or even as a radical critic of political or indeed any other form of morality. The Berlin article runs the tape over Machiavelli in such a spirited way that students tend to become wary of committing to any one of the many schools of interpretation highlighted by Berlin. One advantage of Berlin's very learned commentary is that it discounts the probability that Machiavelli was a model 'scientist' separating fact from the value in a reliably detached way. Berlin argues that Machiavelli is more of a model of a 'political theorist' who rewrites 'value' as a subordinate but core component of effective politics. Berlin foreshadows later interpretations of Machiavelli as a deeply personal theorist whose unsettling rhetoric in *The Prince* reflects his promotion of a committed 'way of life' and not simply a neutral way of thinking (Tarcov 2013; Strauss 1984, 282–284; Skinner 1981, 48–77).

Second, Berlin vigorously promotes his own interpretation which is radical in its own way in identifying Machiavelli as an enthusiast for a new kind of political morality free from traditional restraints external to politics, such as those in religious or ethical doctrine. Berlin's case is alluring because he suggests that Machiavelli is not elevating politics above morality but is, in fact, rewriting morality into his new form of politics, so that morality takes on a new life not as a traditional constraint on politics but as an identifier of what stands out as effective, real politics: acting morally means acting politically for whatever good purposes might have been protected and indeed promoted by Machiavelli.

Third, we find Berlin reading Machiavelli as the founding thinker of modern liberalism who celebrated tolerable regimes of 'choice' (usually identified by Machiavelli as *virtu*) as the recommended political culture of effective modern politics. Yet Berlin's account of Machiavelli's concept of 'choice' comes close to pushing Machiavelli into the postmodern world of the 'will to power', as though Machiavelli was the forefather of

Nietzsche who summoned readers to postmodern greatness by inciting them to go those few steps beyond civic toleration and embrace the fortifying greatness of momentous political leaders prefigured, if in muted form, in many of the examples of 'founders' in *The Prince*.

Berlin's unusual interpretation of Machiavelli helps teachers help students prepare to encounter Machiavelli as a political radical. Machiavelli emerges as the curious case of a thinker for whom there is only politics, and nothing else. Machiavelli has a capacity to render this recovery of political activism as an influential source for the modern world of liberalism and toleration protecting competing agendas of personal choice. But he also has a capacity to act as a deeper source for postmodern activism: Berlin uncovers an uneasiness in many contemporary accounts of Machiavelli, including a kind of postmodern uneasiness about the modesty of political leadership shaped under modern liberalism. Berlin covers two bases, as it were: he summons up Machiavelli as a necessary but insufficient figure in the later system of liberalism's checks and balances; but he also warns readers that Machiavelli's deepest thinking about politics might go much further beyond the comfortable liberalism favoured by later anti-Machiavellians.

This brings us to our final way of making early use of Berlin, which is to help students get some sense of the wider impact of Berlin's interpretation of Machiavelli by considering the sharp and critical commentary Berlin's article provoked from prominent US literature theorist Kenneth Burke (Burke 1972). The value of Burke's very critical reply to Berlin was that Berlin had ignored or at least downplayed Machiavelli's distinctive rhetoric and that this feature of Machiavelli's writing might reveal neglected dimensions of his slyly formulated theory of politics. Burke was generous enough to note the vigour of Berlin's own writing but also tough enough to remind readers that Machiavelli uses his rhetoric to amuse and delight but also to instruct his readers about his deeper purposes. Burke referred readers to a section of his own interpretation of Machiavelli in his recent book *A Rhetoric of Motives*: this account is called '"Administrative" Rhetoric in Machiavelli' examining many examples of Machiavelli's rhetorical arts of writing (Burke 1969, 158–166). Students curious about the place of rhetoric in political theory then have a resource to turn to which, in our view, could bring them closer to the living reality of a classic text like *The Prince*. There is 'something deceptive' about the manner of presentation in *The Prince* (Skinner 1988, xii). As teachers, we advertise this advantage and are happy to discuss Burke's alternative perspectives to any students beginning to show their curiosity about Machiavelli's arts of thinking hidden so deceptively in his arts of writing.

Who First Gets to Read *The Prince*?

Academic teachers of political theory often become the witnesses to groups of students who are invited to read *The Prince* for the first time. Machiavelli spent quite a lot of time on arranging who might be the very first person to read this work. The *Dedicatory Letter* which now occupies the first two pages of *The Prince* was originally intended to be addressed to the son of Lorenzo the Magnificent. Machiavelli later changed this to Lorenzo's grandson: Lorenzo de' Medici (Machiavelli 1998, 3–4; Zuckert 2017, 41–46). In this public letter we see some of the ways that Machiavelli sees his own public role as author of this new text and many of the curious ways that he relates to his readers—including the important readers other than the important member of the Medici clan here identified as the worthy recipient of this work. From Machiavelli's famous letter of 10 December 1513 to Vettori, we learn just how important it was for Machiavelli to persuade 'these Medici lords' to 'begin to make use of me' and to appreciate that *The Prince* is Machiavelli's comprehensive 'study of the art of the state' (Machiavelli 1998, 107–111; Strauss 1984, 74–77; Mansfield 1996, 264–265).

The *Dedicatory Letter* proves a perfect way to begin a course of lectures in the history of modern political theory. Students begin to see a rare example of the performance of a political theorist who uses this public letter to frame the way readers, including contemporary readers today, learn to read the private reconsiderations lodged in this puzzling text. Some critics see the *Dedicatory Letter* as 'a subtle satire' about Lorenzo (Pangle and Burns 2015, 202). Others take it more seriously: of great influence in recent teaching and scholarship has been Viroli's book *Redeeming the Prince* on 'the meaning of Machiavelli's Masterpiece'— which includes a revealing section on the rhetoric used in this *Dedicatory Letter* as an example of the type of deliberative rhetoric to expect subsequently in this text (Viroli 2014, 98–108). Viroli notes that many interpreters of Machiavelli take for granted what is stated in this Letter— assuming that Machiavelli is right when he explicitly states that he will avoid the arts of rhetoric in the main body of the text. To the contrary, Viroli states that Machiavelli carefully applies 'the rules of deliberative rhetoric' intended to make the text as persuasive as possible in the political advice it provides. Curtly put in the opening letter, but more expansively deployed in the 26 chapters to follow, readers can expect to find endless examples of such rhetorical devices as similes, images, metaphors and above all 'the technique of irony' intended to deride as it belittles and censures Machiavelli's opponents (Viroli 2014, 100–101).

The suggestion to students is that the *Dedicatory Letter* is not simply for show. The substance of the relationship between author and reader is here on display. Lorenzo's reading as a powerful office holder is not necessarily the reading the author wants all readers, especially those not holding office, to take. The 'new prince' might be watching on, slowly reading the text presented by Machiavelli to Lorenzo. The Letter begins with the phrase 'it is customary' when describing the conduct of those 'acquiring favor' (typically patronage but here it could be publicity) who go out of their way to make gifts to 'a Prince'. Most of *The Prince* is about bypassing or overcoming 'custom' in order to 'acquire favor'. Machiavelli states that he is about to break custom right here in the first paragraph because he is not going to present Lorenzo with customary gifts. Instead, the author will present a small book about 'the knowledge of the actions of great men'. This knowledge is itself uncustomary—drawn up in 'one small volume' from 'long experience' of modern things and 'continuous reading' of ancient things. Thus we learn that *The Prince* is a work of 'knowledge', so that we readers have to ask if we—or indeed Lorenzo—have whatever it takes to understand that 'knowledge' (Tarcov 2013, 102–106).

Machiavelli writes in the *Dedicatory Letter* that his book is a great gift to present, so long as the receiver has 'the capacity to be able to understand' all that is understood by the author. The phrasing here is confusing in that it almost suggests that the author's life of 'hardship and dangers' has helped him learn to understand what might be hard to understand for those used to customary ways. Adding to the author's war against custom is the declaration that this work lacks the customary adornments of fancy rhetoric. Instead, Machiavelli hopes that the work will be pleased on account of its 'variety' and indeed 'gravity'. Fearing it might be presumptuous for one so low to 'discuss and give rules' for those in high office, Machiavelli invokes the parallel tale of sketchers and knowers: those on high can sketch and know 'low places' but those lowly ones alone can sketch and know 'the nature of princes'. Somewhat surprisingly for this seeker after 'favor', the author states that the low are 'of the people'—as though Lorenzo and his likes are holders of princely office but yet to prove that they are in fact 'princes' who can really claim to know 'the natures of peoples'. The task now becomes how well Lorenzo and his likes will, to use Machiavelli's careful terminology, read the text 'diligently' and how likely it is that these conventional princes will act to remove 'the malignity of fortune' from Machiavelli (Machiavelli 1998, 3–4).

THE NEW PRINCE AT THE END OF *THE PRINCE*

Students new to *The Prince* like to compare the opening Letter with the last chapter which seems to carry the hot fervour of Machiavelli's call for a new prince (Machiavelli 1998, 101–105; Strauss 1984, 62–69). Viroli's *Redeeming the Prince* makes great use of this final chapter to prove that it is not a late-addition to a previously completed work but is, in fact, the rhetorical culmination of the whole work (Viroli 2014, 108–112). This last chapter is entitled in part an 'Exhortation' which allows students to see Machiavelli advocating in his most extreme form—and thereby revealing to his readers much that they should know about turning theory into practice. The full title refers to an exhortation to 'seize Italy' and 'to free her from the barbarians'. The practical focus might tempt readers to think that Machiavelli's 'rhetoric' in the end comes down to a form of patriotism or what was later called nationalism. The term 'Italy' never really came to national fruition until the nineteenth century, so the usual description is of Machiavelli being a forerunner of Italian nationalism. The reference to 'barbarians' seems usually understood by new students of *The Prince* to mean 'non-Italians': academic teachers can easily get some distance with this patriotic interpretation.

Yet many critics see something more. Viroli, for instance, notes that *The Prince* 'ends with Machiavelli's silence' (Viroli 2014, 110). He means in part that the end of this final chapter is a quotation from Petrarch's *My Italy* calling on a revival of Italian valour and virtue (Machiavelli 1998, 105). Viroli also means that Machiavelli leaves unsaid what he himself really identifies as the cause or greater purpose of valour and virtue: Italian nationalism might well be that greater purpose but there is very little praise for Italian nationality in the preceding 25 chapters in *The Prince*. Most of the preceding discussion has been about a form of government (principalities) and a form of ruler (princes). A prominent theme has been this idea of a 'new prince' where that is presented as a new *idea* about princes and not simply yet another new occupant of a princely office (Mansfield 1996, 31–36).

It can help students if they see that this last chapter contains two quotations: the final one from Petrarch and an earlier one from Livy, used when Machiavelli wants to summon up the justice of the cause facing the 'new prince' who will redeem Italy from the 'barbarous cruelties and insults' (Machiavelli 1998, 102–103). The Livy quote includes the statement that 'war is just to whom it is necessary' and goes on to say that 'arms are pious when there is not hope but in arms'. The story which follows in the next few sentences adapts the struggle of Moses as a convincing account of what can be achieved if there is 'very great readiness' to tackle 'extraordinary things'. Although Machiavelli addresses this to 'your illustrious house' of the Medici (a phrase used four times in five paragraphs) where Lorenzo's uncle has taken over as pope and 'is now prince', readers have to measure this potential redeemer against the weight of the task identified by Machiavelli. It is not immediately clear whether the most significant 'barbarous cruelties and insults' are committed solely by non-Italians, or whether only Italians can arouse 'the virtue of an Italian spirit'.

Students can be pleasantly puzzled when invited to examine the concluding chapter as a rhetorical reframing of Machiavelli's ideas about newness in the role of a prince. Rhetoric here does not mean, as many students tend to think, ways of disguising Machiavelli's real thoughts so that they can slip past his readers; instead, rhetoric here means something very similar to what classical students of rhetoric (like Aristotle in his *Rhetoric*) thought it meant, which is the art of persuasion from author to reader—or perhaps from author to those particularly astute readers who Machiavelli hopes to persuade to carry on his work begun, but barely completed, in the 26 chapters of *The Prince* (Zuckert 2017, 101–107).

Much depends then on how readers interpret the nature of the new prince which dominates the concluding chapter. The first sentence of this last chapter refers twice to 'a new prince' who might indeed emerge initially as 'someone prudent and virtuous'—but not yet a prince. The examples then listed by Machiavelli are all great founders who emerged from the 'ruin' of subjugated peoples not unlike Italy: the 'virtue' of Moses, the 'greatness of spirit' of Cyrus, the 'excellence' of Theseus—but we note Machiavelli's silence about the role of Romulus who was included in the earlier chapter examining these great founders (Machiavelli 1998, 101–102; cf. Chap. 6: 21–25). Machiavelli states that he is searching for 'the virtue of an Italian spirit' yet he fails here to mention Romulus, the founder of Rome, in his review of those 'rare and marvellous' leaders of times past. Our teaching experience is that it helps to alert students to this old prince, precisely because he might reveal something important about what is present or what is missing in the 'new prince' dominating the author's attention. The quotation from Livy might occupy special importance if it is one of the few references to Rome in this patriotic chapter.

The central paragraph in this concluding chapter dampens whatever enthusiasm the house of Medici might have had or wanted to have for their role as redeemers. The paragraph notes the defect of 'ancient orders' in Italy and the very real importance of 'a man' who can 'found' what are called 'new laws and the new orders' deserved by Italy. But the theme is that Italy is not yet ready to refound itself: Italian armies when composed entirely of their own people suffer defeat after defeat, reflecting 'the weakness at the head' in the absence of real leadership. The 'new prince' identified in the fourth paragraph does not seem to be a Medici who are modelled against 'those excellent men' (who remain unnamed, unless we mean Moses, Cyrus and Theseus) who 'with Italian virtue' can command through a 'regeneration of arms and a change in orders' (Machiavelli 1998, 104–105). The final paragraph ends with the Petrarch quotation as the preferred way of concluding this discussion of the 'barbarian domination' threatening 'this fatherland'. Machiavelli uses one of his rare formulation of 'love' as he evokes the kind of reception awaiting the 'redeemer' deserving the 'homage' of all Italians.

Performing like a Prince

One of the most pressing challenges facing those trying to teach students about Machiavelli's *The Prince* is to let them see that the work is curiously incomplete. The work is relatively brief, so it is not too hard for students to think that Machiavelli might well have had more to say about politics—which is clearly true as students learn about the wide range of works by Machiavelli, most larger and denser, or rather more diversified, than *The Prince* (Strauss 1984, 32–48). Our view is that Machiavelli was rightly proud of his performance in writing *The Prince*: proud, that is, that the work was as well constructed as possible for those readers with the kind of 'diligence' noted in the *Dedicatory Letter* who could learn how to transform the 'knowledge' identified in the Letter into something more like a theory or doctrine about politics. Machiavelli's intentionally short work is like a starter kit for those willing to learn how to think about politics as Machiavelli thinks about politics (Viroli 2000, 153–161).

Two aspects of the cagy incompleteness of *The Prince* relate to the idea of the new prince and it is these two aspects which teachers can use to help students get further into Machiavelli's somewhat hidden theories about politics. The first aspect is roughly half way between the *Dedicatory Letter* and the final chapter: this is the oddly brief two paragraph chapter 15 about why princes are 'praised or blamed' (Machiavelli 1998, 61–62). This surprisingly compact chapter provides readers with what we can take as a general model of the new prince so that we get a feel for the type being cultivated or promoted by Machiavelli. The second aspect is perhaps Machiavelli's most noted example of a case study of a prince in *The Prince*: this is the set of quite a few portraits and studies of Cesare Borgia which many critics take as evidence of Machiavelli's preferred example of the type of new prince he favoured. The very hard task facing those teaching *The Prince* is to help students learn the 'theory', as it were, in chapter 15 and apply it to the Borgia case study presented over many chapters by Machiavelli. It turns out that Machiavelli probably did intend to use the Borgia case study to clarify the nature of the new prince—but this might also mean that Borgia too has something missing or incomplete in his princely makeup which students have to read through as they follow Machiavelli's performance as a public instructor (Namejy 2013; Orwin 2016).

The detail compressed into the short chapter 15 is impressive. The second sentence notes that Machiavelli fears 'I may be held presumptuous' for writing about rule; a similar fear of presumption occurred in the *Dedicatory Letter* (Machiavelli 1998, 4, 61). The original fear now finds its mark in this later chapter where Machiavelli rewrites the rules for ruling. The chapters which follow spell out the implications at some length, but the start of the story is the directly personal encounter Machiavelli makes in chapter 15. Many critics contend that Machiavelli typically speaks indirectly to his readers. Yet this chapter opens with a statement about what 'to see' in the 'modes and government of a prince'. The second sentence contains four uses of the word 'I' as Machiavelli surprisingly discloses a personal preference to 'depart from the orders of others' who have written about princely modes (Tarcov 2013). This departure begins with what he 'sees': it 'has appeared to me' to try to be 'useful' by going 'directly to the effectual truth' rather than 'to the imagination' of that truth. Many traditional models of perfect rule 'have never been seen'. Then comes a blunt assertion of what he sees: those who strive to do 'what should be done' achieve 'ruin' rather than 'preservation'. Thus 'it is necessary' for those who want 'to maintain' themselves 'to learn to be able not to be good' whenever necessary (Machiavelli 1998, 61; Lefort 2000, 109–141).

The second paragraph examines praise and blame. Machiavelli invites his readers to consider a lengthy set of 'qualities' which can be held to be praiseworthy or blameworthy. The implication is along the lines we noted from Berlin: ruling well means making hard choices which some will see as virtuous and others will see as vicious (Zuckert 2017, 78). The task is not to be either virtuous or vicious but to be an effective chooser of whatever option will prove more useful. The general rule is that necessity requires that a ruler 'be so prudent' as to 'avoid the infamy' of whatever vices he might have to use: which here means that a ruler 'should not care' about that infamy if those vices help 'save one's state' and so achieves 'one's security and well-being' (Machiavelli 1998, 62). There are many case studies in *The Prince* which throw light on how this 'theory' works in practice. Teachers know that their job is on target when students eagerly debate their competing models of which rulers they think best illustrate Machiavelli's idea of a new prince. Could it be Moses or Cyrus or Theseus or Romulus or Agathocles or Hannibal or Severus or Hiero or even Lorenzo, receiver of the *Dedicatory Letter*? The one example worth examining here is Cesare Borgia because his tale can tell students much about the style and the substance of Machiavelli's *The Prince* (Pangle and Burns 2015, 209–214; Orwin 2016).

Performing like Cesare Borgia

Lorenzo and Borgia share something important: they both have a pope as a near relative. It is quite possible that Machiavelli wants to make something from this similar relationship with a pope. Borgia's father had been a pope and with his death much seems to vanish from the cause marshalled by Borgia. Lorenzo has an uncle who is a later pope and it is possible that this second relationship can learn to overcome whatever limitations might be discerned in the earlier relationship (Zuckert 2017, 60). Raising these sort of puzzles helps students begin to see the power of the papacy in Machiavelli's world of politics. Thinking through all the implications of both relationships might clarify the role Machiavelli held for the papacy in the political future—if such a role exists, contrary to the view of some critics of Machiavelli's deeply held anti-Christianity (Scott and Sullivan 1994).

In *The Prince*, Borgia appears under two names: usually he is *Cesare Borgia* but sometimes he is *Valentino* or *the duke of Valentino* or simply *the duke*. This man with two names stands out as a man with two or more personalities, which suggests something ambiguous about what Machiavelli might consider his central persona or his integrity. The first appearance of Borgia in *The Prince* is almost in passing towards the end of chapter 3 where Machiavelli describes him as 'Valentino'—noting that this is how he was called 'by the people' (Machiavelli 1998, 16). This description is varied when we next encounter Borgia which is in chapter 7 when he is described as 'Duke Valentino by the vulgar' (Machiavelli 1998, 26–27). The third and final reference to duke Valentino occurs in chapter 11 where 'the duke' is mentioned three times, simply as an instrument of Pope Alexander VI, with all the praise placed on the ambitious pope rather than on his usually clever instrument (Machiavelli 1998, 46–47). This is the diminished picture of Borgia, highlighted by his elevated relationship with people who, apparently alone and without support from other leading figures, hold him high as 'the duke' (Orwin 2016).

Machiavelli's own estimate emerges particularly in chapter 7 dealing with rule through two important externalities or dependencies often sought by princes: the arms of others and fortune. In many ways, *The Prince* has as one of its core theses that effective rule really depends as little as possible on either of these externalities: it is better to rule through the use of one's own arms and not to rely or depend on fortune. The fact that Borgia emerges so prominently in this chapter could mean that he illustrates the type of prince whose power and effectiveness is ultimately held back by either an inability to command his own arms or by the inability to manage fortune and especially misfortune which Machiavelli argues, especially in the second last chapter which is mainly about 'fortune', is a classic test of the *virtu* of new prince (Machiavelli 1998, 98–101; Zuckert 2017, 60–64).

The important point here is that teachers can use Machiavelli's curiously cautious praise of Borgia as a very useful way of helping students learn how to read the mind of Machiavelli by learning more about how to read the puzzling text of this influential political theorist. Chapter 7 opens with a critical examination of those princes who arise and later fall through the passage of fortune which tends to produce 'very inconstant and unstable things'. The message is that only princes with 'great ingenuity and virtue', indeed 'so much virtue', can establish their own 'foundations' which can not only benefit from good fortune but also resist the inevitable surge of bad fortune. Who illustrates this kind of 'great ingenuity'? Machiavelli invites readers to consider two contemporary examples: the successful rule of Sforza and the ultimately unsuccessful example of one of Sforza's rivals, Borgia. Borgia is the one signalled out by Machiavelli as a 'prudent and virtuous' ruler who depended greatly on 'the fortune of his father' and who went on to establish 'great foundations'—at least for his 'future power'. But 'his orders' failed him: Machiavelli explains that 'it was not his fault' that he was ruined by an 'extreme malignity of fortune'. Or so at least it seems: speaking personally, Machiavelli says that 'I do not know what better teaching I could give to a new prince than this example of his actions' (Machiavelli 1998, 25–27; Orwin 2016, 165–170).

The 'example' is complicated, with Machiavelli writing about a wide range of historical details about the rise of 'the duke' into greatness as a ruler, urged on effectively by his father who was Pope Alexander VI. Students here have a wonderful opportunity to descend into the level of detail favoured by Machiavelli, who knows that every norm or rule in politics is dependent on a wealth of circumstances, not all of which can be commanded by all those competing for rule. Students have to read with great care to decide how much of Borgia's elevation to greatness rested on actions of his father and how much on Borgia's own actions. What dominates this treatment is Machiavelli's description of Borgia's steadily growing determination to lessen his dependence on the arms of others, so that we can see 'the greatness of the duke' displayed in his divide and rule strategies against his untrustworthy friends as well as distrustful opponents, and the use of 'deceit' and capacity 'to dissimulate' in order to establish 'very good foundations for his power' (Machiavelli 1998, 27–29; Namejy 2013).

Among the many positives identified by Machiavelli with Borgia, one is 'deserving of notice and of being imitated by others' (Machiavelli 1998, 29). When taking over Romagna, Borgia introduced his own system of 'good government' to repair the disrepair of its selfish but incapable former rulers. Included in this scheme was the appointment of Remirro, 'a cruel and ready man', who imposed unity on the region 'with the very greatest reputation for himself'. Fearing that this 'excessive authority' might generate 'hateful' relationships with the people, Borgia again engaged in a form of 'good government' through the establishment of a court of inquiry into the 'cruelty' practised by minister Remirro. Borgia seized Remirro and placed him, in a public square, 'in two pieces': Machiavelli states that the 'ferocity of this spectacle left the people at once satisfied and stupefied' (Machiavelli 1998, 30).

Among the negatives are a series of confusing indecisions revolving around the theme of what 'if Alexander had lived'—to use Machiavelli's fascinating language (Machiavelli 1998, 30). It appears that Machiavelli thinks that Borgia 'would soon have succeeded' in his quest for stronger foundations if only his father had not died. In relation to one very long paragraph, teachers can ask students to evaluate what they think Machiavelli really thinks of Borgia's 'arrangements', given what Borgia had begun 'to fear' about rivalry from whoever became the new pope. The long paragraph is an excellent example of Machiavelli's educational rhetoric which forces readers to instruct themselves well by thinking beyond the black letters on the page. The text contains a wealth of detail about what Borgia 'thought' about what conduct he should perform after his father's death. While it might appear that 'there was such ferocity and such virtue in the duke', the facts tell another story: that his 'foundations' were far from complete and that his own health was dwindling so much that he was 'on the point of dying'. Here Machiavelli makes one of the few uses in *The Prince* where he relates things told to him by others—in this case, by Borgia. The reported comment was at the time of the assumption to papal office of Julius II, as though that event dealt a very bad blow to Borgia's rule (Machiavelli 1998, 32).

The final paragraph of chapter 7 begins with Machiavelli's claim that Borgia should be imitated and concludes with Machiavelli's statement that 'his ultimate ruin' reflected a single 'bad choice'—which was to allow the appointment of Julius II as the new pope. Read more closely, the paragraph says that Borgia should only be imitated by those who depend on fortune and the force of other's arms; and that Borgia's 'bad choice' of not stopping Julius II being appointed should not be imitated by those who have to manage around or live with or tolerate the papacy. Within these limits, it might be true that one 'can find no fresher examples than the actions' of Borgia; and within these limits, there is a long list of admirable qualities reflected well in the rule of Borgia. The chapter closes with many of the strengths and weaknesses identified, but with a growing suspicion among readers that Machiavelli might be making the case against this type of model of a new prince, instead of making the case for Borgia at all (Orwin 2016, 162–165).

CONCLUSION

Terse as is *The Prince*, there is more to follow on Borgia. In fact, there are five more accounts of Borgia which add depth to Machiavelli's portrait of this great but limited prince. My interest here is in helping teachers see their role in promoting students to become detectives as they deepen their initial reading of this work. What does it mean to hear of Borgia's deception and strangling of Liverotto, or to hear of Borgia's high reputation when he eventually eliminated his reliance on the arms of allies and became 'the total owner of his own arms', or to hear of Borgia's bad reputation for cruelty when in fact his rule of Romagna was an example of cruelty well used, or to hear of Borgia's avoidance of popular hatred when overcoming the protection of fortresses (Machiavelli 1998, 37, 55, 65, 86–87)?

Teaching students about Machiavelli can begin by teaching them how to read *The Prince* as 'a kind of playful dialogue' between the theorist as educator and readers as potential new princes (Pangle and Burns 2015, 199). Included in this dialogue are examples where Machiavelli shows his readers some of the arts he uses when reading important books dealing with political theory. The author becomes a model for his readers: one important example is in chapter 14 where Machiavelli reflects on 'the exercise of the mind', where we see how the great prince Scipio learned from his close reading of Xenophon's life of Cyrus; another example is in chapter 17 where we learn more about Scipio's 'fame and glory' which looms large as a life well read; and another example appears in chapter 18 where Machiavelli describes the ways that 'ancient writers' were able to teach 'covertly to princes' through rhetorical strategies worth recovering by those readers now wanting either to learn about or even become new princes (Machiavelli 1998, 60, 68, 69; Strauss 1984, 58–61, 292–294; Mansfield 1996, 295–314).

REFERENCES

Berlin, Isaiah. 1969. Two Concepts of Liberty. In *Four Essays on Liberty*. Oxford: Oxford University Press.

Berlin, Isaiah. 1971. The Question of Machiavelli. *New York Review of Books*, November.
Burke, Kenneth. 1969. *A Rhetoric of Motives*. Berkeley: University of California Press.
Burke, Kenneth. 1972. Exchange on Machiavelli. *New York Review of Books*, April.
De Grazia, Sebastian. 1996. *Machiavelli in Hell*. London: Papermac.
Lefort, Claude. 2000. *Writing: The Political Test*. Durham, NC: Duke University Press.
Machiavelli, N. 1998. *The Prince*. Translated and with an Introduction by Harvey C. Mansfield, 2nd ed. Chicago: University of Chicago Press.
Mansfield, Harvey C. 1996. *Machiavelli's Virtue*. Chicago: University of Chicago Press.
Namejy, John M. 2013. Machiavelli and Cesare Borgia: A Reconsideration of Chapter 7 of *The Prince*. *Review of Politics* 75 (x): 539–556.
Orwin, Clifford. 2016. The Riddle of Cesare Borgia and the Legacy of Machiavelli's Prince. In *Machiavelli's Legacies: The Prince after Five Hundred Years*, ed. Timothy Fuller, 156–170. Philadelphia: University of Pennsylvania Press.
Pangle, Thomas, and Timothy Burns. 2015. *The Key Texts of Political Philosophy: An Introduction*. New York: Cambridge University Press.
Scott, John T., and Vickie B. Sullivan. 1994. Patricide and the Plot of the Prince: Cesare Borgia and Machiavelli's Italy. *American Political Science Review* 88 (4): 887–900.
Skinner, Quentin. 1981. *Machiavelli*. Oxford: Oxford University Press.
Skinner, Quentin. 1988. Introduction. In *Machiavelli's The Prince*, ed. Quentin Skinner and Russell Price. Cambridge: Cambridge University Press.
Strauss, Leo. 1984. *Thoughts on Machiavelli*. Midway Reprint. Chicago: University of Chicago Press.
Tarcov, Nathan. 2013. Machiavelli in *The Prince*: His Way of Life in Question. In *Political Philosophy Cross-Examined*, ed. Thomas L. Pangle and J. Harvey Lomax, 100–118. New York: Palgrave.
Viroli, Maurizio. 2000. *Niccolo's Smile: A Biography of Machiavelli*. Translated from the Italian by Antony Shugaar. New York: Farrar, Straus and Giroux.
Viroli, Maurizio. 2014. *Redeeming the Prince: The Meaning of Machiavelli's Masterpiece*. Princeton: Princeton University Press.
Zuckert, Catherine H. 2017. *Machiavelli's Politics*. Chicago: University of Chicago Press.

CHAPTER 5

Reading J. S. Mill's *On Liberty*

Performing as a Citizen

Abstract The fourth lesson comes from J. S. Mill. *On Liberty* is a core text in modern liberal theory. Why is this text so hotly debated? The answer is that Mill wanted his text to be hotly debated: this is his way of re-educating his readers into new theories of political liberty.

Keywords Mill · Harriet Mill · Female suffrage · Individuality
Virtue · Excellence

'Liberty' is a key term in modern political thought, so it is no surprise that one of the later champions of liberal political theory should use this term as the title of what became perhaps his most famous text. Readers of *On Liberty* are right to ask what type of liberty this work examines: is it *individual* or *civil* liberty or perhaps *both* types? A related question is whether these types of liberty are means or ends of politics: is the purpose of politics to promote these liberties as ends in themselves, requiring limited systems of government; or to promote them as, in normal circumstances, the most effective means to generate the substantive ends of politics, such as the common good or, to use one of Mill's related reform doctrines from a companion work *Utilitarianism*: 'social and distributive justice' (Mill 1991b, 198)?

The reference to 'performing as a citizen' reflects Mill's very deep interest in citizenship. Mill's *On Liberty* is itself a civic performance written by Mill (either alone or with help from his wife) dedicated to citizenship: the models of fuller individuality promoted in this work are examples of active citizenship. The type of individualism being cultivated by Mill matches in many ways his own style of civic performance where he as a prominent individual speaks and acts out without, at least until elected to the House of Commons in 1865, holding any particular public office. Mill's *On Liberty* examines the civic use of liberties by excellent citizens who can nurture and shape the civic culture of a more deliberative democracy than Britain's then-current system of representative government. Rulers most certainly perform important roles in political systems; but Mill insists that so too do those who are ruled, many of whom can make their own distinctive contributions to the well-being of the polity.

The Two Mills

To read any of Mill's longer 'essays' means that we encounter debate over 'what Mill really meant' by his argument in this or that work of political theory. Our fear is that many new students coming to Mill get distracted by the proliferation of often-simplistic debate over the various interpretations of Mill. In the case of those starting to read *On Liberty*, these debates have grown into a life of their own, with students having to choose between trying their own hand at making sense of Mill's presentation of five chapters covering around 110 pages (see e.g. edited selections in Bailey 2012, 627–652; and the whole text in Mill 2015). An alternative choice is to take their cues from one or more of the many available summaries of what some interpreters think Mill might have meant—or indeed what Mill failed to make clear in all those 110 pages of opaque argument. *On Liberty* covers many topics in politics and public policy, which has stimulated many generations of commentators to propose their own interpretations of what they take to be Mill's core thesis (see e.g. Mill 2015, 185–200).

Two long-standing contentions are that Mill's core argument was about the relative merits of 'positive' and 'negative' liberty (Berlin in Bailey 2012, 797–823). The focus on liberty as an end is very much like what later theorists following Berlin have called a 'negative' concept of the value of liberty obtained where we have 'freedom from' authority expressed through virtues of individualism. Alternatively, the focus on liberty as a means is more like a 'positive' concept of the value of liberty obtained where we have 'freedom to' cultivate some form of communitarianism expressed through civic solidarity.

Mill's reputation for *On Liberty* is probably more divided than is his reputation for his other works. The famous account of the 'two Mills' comes out of *On Liberty*'s curiously indistinct relationship between one theme of the core value of a somewhat eccentric individuality and another theme of the core value of social solidarity (Himmelfarb 1963, vii–xxiv; 1985, 7–49). The problem for teachers of Mill's most acknowledged work of political theory is that their potential audience starts with a version of this division between those who are ready to have confirmed their view of Mill as a theorist of individualism and those in contrast seeking evidence of Mill's theory of sociality or even communitarianism. The awkward problem is that so few scholars of *On Liberty* can present a coherent account of a unified teaching overcoming these two commonly identified themes (Himmelfarb 2006, 94–120).

My own approach is to put aside these swirls of debate and to turn directly to the work itself, hoping that Mill as author has 'performed' with sufficient clarity that we can audit the work in the ways we think he originally intended. It might be that we discover that this pathway matches one of the many schools of interpretation now circulating; or it might be that we discover that Mill's best efforts at guiding his readers have escaped many of his later noisy followers; or it might be that we are very misguided to think that we can recover Mill's original intentions. On this last point, it is worth noting that Mill's *Autobiography* is a profitable potential source for those reading *On Liberty* (Mill 2015, 177–183). Mill's story of his own intellectual life was published after his death in 1873, nearly a decade and a half after the publication in 1859 of *On Liberty*. The autobiography has an insightful review of *On Liberty* which we will use towards the end of this chapter.

Reading *On Liberty*

What we find when we open *On Liberty* (even editions crowded with appendices sampling the heated debates over the meaning of the text) is an epigraph from the German philosopher von Humboldt who is later quoted four times in *On Liberty*: twice in chapter 4 and twice in chapter 5 (Mill 2015, 43, 97–98, 112, 141–142, 145). The initial quote refers to the value of 'human development in its richest diversity' as illustrated in this work. This helps us identify a theme for *On Liberty* which is not simply individuality as an option but rather the 'development' of humanity which could well draw on some notion of human excellence or virtue as a model of development. This notion returns in the second quotation where von Humboldt is quoted in relation to the developed powers of a human being as 'a complete and consistent whole'. The quoted text then turns to 'the individuality' of such development which rests on 'two requisites': one is 'freedom' and the other is 'a variety of situations' (later detailed at pp. 112–113 as a declining circumstance in modern democracies) which, when united, produce 'originality'. Mill devotes some very important pages to 'originality' which might even be a self-portrait given that Mill elevates it to line up with 'genius', defined as that rare and socially valuable 'freedom to point out the way' to others. When describing the importance of 'exceptional individuals', Mill counter-balances against the conventional sway of 'collective mediocrity' his puzzling alternative of 'eccentricity'. Mill even states that 'the chief danger of the time' is that 'so few' of those with 'strength of character' think they can or should 'dare to be eccentric' (see e.g. Mill 2015, 98, 104–107).

We will come back to this theme of character later, but the important point here is that Mill is defending 'eccentricity' in very special terms: he is highlighting the 'highly gifted and instructed One or Few' who have the power of 'genius' to break ranks from, and potentially provide political leadership to, 'the sovereign Many' who cling to the 'collective mediocrity' which is 'the ascendant power among mankind'.

The second last citation of von Humboldt relates to the subject of marriage which is indeed the subject of the special paragraph on page one of the text. The language here is about moral responsibilities in marriage which in turn relate to 'the *legal* freedom' enjoyed by both parties to cease the marriage (Mill 2015, 141–142). Mill's language here invites readers to wonder about circumstances where a marriage partner might use their legal freedom to cease a marriage if they think the other party had failed to uphold their moral responsibilities. The importance of this issue for Mill will be examined very shortly when we see how importantly Mill identifies his own wife's moral responsibility as his co-author. The final reference to von Humboldt refers to education certification where Mill signals his agreement that governments should not have the power to award or limit awards of competency for those who pass independent tests of merit. Governments can facilitate training and certification but they should not hold the power to deny certification to someone considered undesirable, even though competent.

The reference to moral responsibilities in marriage is an important one for Mill. The single dedicatory paragraph is a formal dedication to Mill's recently deceased wife Harriet Taylor who is reported to be 'in part the author, of all that is best in my writings' (Mill 2015, 43). Mill first met Harriet in 1830 when she was married to her first husband, who died in 1849. Mill married Harriet in 1851; she died in 1858, the year before the publication of *On Liberty*. Mill dedicates 'this volume' to Harriet who is described in his *Autobiography* as a person of 'genius' (Mill 1991b, 146). Further, Mill acknowledges in his dedication that this work 'belongs as much to her as to me'. It would seem that Mill here means that 'her revision' and 're-examination' improved his writing through the application of her 'unrivaled wisdom' (Mill 2015, 43). Mill admits this as a source of his inability in that he does not know what wisdom she might have taken with her at her death. Mill says that his 'benefit' to the world would be much greater if he were capable of interpreting her thoughts to the world at large. It could be that in the absence of that capability, Mill knows that he cannot offer that 'greater benefit' the two authors together could provide.

Readers now begin to look over the stated arrangement listed in the table of contents: five chapters are listed, a model followed in Mill's later 'essay' *Utilitarianism* which is an important companion 'essay' to *On Liberty* (Mill 1991a, 131–201). The first and last chapters of *On Liberty* have relatively simple titles: 'Introductory' and 'Applications'. These comparatively brief chapters frame the longer chapters, which cover in general terms 'liberty', 'individuality' and 'authority'. The central chapter examines 'individuality' but we see from the full title that it is about a special type of individuality which serves 'as one of the elements of well-being'. Contemporary readers easily learn that 'well-being' can be interpreted individually or socially or together as related elements of human development. Sure enough, the Mill literature has streams of commentary about 'what Mill really meant' by this concept of 'well-being', with some reducing Mill's argument to a version of libertarianism and others inflating it to a version of socialism: once again, the 'two-Mills' story of internally competing narratives which run the risk of robbing the work of its intellectual integrity.

Mill's Pedagogy

My approach is to see the sequence of chapters as a rhetorically interesting experiment by Mill to devise a new way of thinking about character—which is also a term lending itself to two potentially competing narratives, with one relating to individual character and the other to community character. I think that Mill has both references in mind and that *On Liberty* is an extensive 'essay' on reforming relationships between individual and community character. The 'liberty' being advocated is Mill's own reflective version of the ideally developed virtues of human individuality and human sociality. I say 'ideally' because I see Mill as a proponent of something as substantial as democratic regime change, with *On Liberty* breaking ground as a formulation for the increasingly public role Mill was committing himself to after his wife's death: the decade begun by *On Liberty* has Mill ever more publicly engaged in rethinking and even reactivating the modern democratic regime, through such politically reformist work as *Utilitarianism* and *Considerations on Representative Government* (both 1861), *August Comte and Positivism* (1865), elected to the House of Commons (1865–1868) and the publication ten years after *On Liberty* with his *Subjection of Women* (1869).

Mill's time as an elected member of parliament gave him the important opportunity to propose a motion for women's suffrage in relation to the proposed Second Reform Act on electoral reform. This motion was defeated but it did mark the first substantial attempt by the British parliament to grant the franchise to women. Mill's later *Subjection of Women* is notably significant in that Mill claims it reflects Harriet's 'teachings'—as Mill reports in ways very similar to the dedication to *On Liberty*. Mill's version is that he had very much accepted the case for the equality of women well before he met Harriet, but that she had persuaded him how to relate this issue to the larger theme of 'human improvement' (Mill 1991a, 147, note 8). The two works are also similar in that the *Subjection of Women* not only reflects the thoughts of Mill's deceased wife but also includes the writing of her daughter who was so close to Mill. It is notable that the last work of writing mentioned in Mill's *Autobiography* is this work in support of women's suffrage (Mill 1991a, 168, 185).

The implication we make is that *On Liberty* has important things to say about women as well as men, and that in so doing it frames or opens up Mill's remarkably constructive decade as an influential political actor and advocate. We also see *On Liberty* as deliberately and carefully rhetorical in composition, reflecting Mill's experienced judgment about the obstacles which 'public opinion' would generate to deflect his reformist agenda. Mill's critique of the deadening influence of public opinion clearly reflects some of the influence Alexis de Tocqueville had on Mill's mature thinking about dominating aspects of modern democratic regimes. But we take this French influence back somewhat further than most commentators and note Mill's special acknowledgement of the political theory of Rousseau which is one of the neglected features of *On Liberty*. This reference to Rousseau occurs in the very long second chapter on liberty. Mill had just earlier examined Socrates as an unusual promoter of liberty who had resisted existing conformity and thereafter been executed for his non-conformity. Mill then examines 'the paradoxes of Rousseau' as a quite recent eighteenth-century example of liberal non-conformism attacking 'the compact mass of one-sided opinion' in his time (Mill 2015, 88). The suggestion is that the kind of liberty treasured by Mill depends substantially on 'eccentrics' like Socrates and Rousseau—and possibly J. S. Mill—who resist ruling conformity even though they know how powerful it will be in counter-resisting such opponents. Mill's personal conclusion seems to be that his own critique of ruling opinion must be elusive in order to be effective: his critique has to anticipate the power of the counter-punch and so deflect that antagonistic force through the ruse of his own public rhetoric. Mill is thus acting very politically by deciding to act very unpolitically, that is with surprising guile, in his contest against sovereign conformity.

New students of Mill do not need to know that much about Mill's long-standing interest in rhetoric as a core feature of politics. One fascinating source of this interest is revealed in his early essay on Plato's dialogue *Gorgias*, one of many Platonic dialogues studied carefully by the youthful Mill (Mill 1965, 75–77). What emerges across these early studies is Mill's preoccupation with Socrates as one of Plato's most instructive characters. It is not surprising that this figure so closely associated with ironic communication should feature so prominently in so many of Mill's later works. It does not take long for even new students to begin to see that Mill might well have devised his own form of irony as central to his own style of rhetoric. Even more significant evidence of Mill's cultivation of his own craft of rhetoric comes from his so-called literary essays and his personal diary (Alexander 1967). Professor Alexander identifies Mill as one of many nineteenth-century examiners of 'culture and democracy' where his special attention to individuality reflects his preoccupation with the special class or category of *cultivated* individuals like Socrates and Rousseau—and we think J. S. Mill—who could enrich democracy and especially its underlying political or civic culture through their rare individuality or eccentricity or genius.

Misreading *On Liberty*

Mill reacted to one of his friendly critics who thought that *On Liberty* was part of a movement for elitism: 'on the contrary' retorted Mill, his aim was 'to make the many more accessible to all the truth by making them more open-minded' (quoted Alexander 1967, xx). Readers who think that *On Liberty* reflects Mill as a libertarian will be surprised to find that his real preference was for we now call liberal democracy: that is, for the civil liberty of a cohesive political community of equally entitled citizens devoted to a civic culture of human excellence. A *liberal* democracy is not so much a democracy liberated from anti-democratic misrule as a democracy committed to liberal concepts of civic excellence, which *On Liberty* exemplifies. Through his literary works, including we insist *On Liberty*, Mill sought ways to promote the 'cultivation of goodness and nobleness and the hope of their ultimate entire ascendancy' (quoted Alexander 1967, xxix).

How then can we encourage students to navigate their way through *On Liberty* and learn as Mill wanted them to learn? The work is too long for students to tackle it through a quick read and it is too densely organised for them to tease out core ideas from secondary analyses of related themes. We think it helps readers if they are alerted to what we think is Mill's core idea which slowly solidifies as the work unfolds: this idea is *character*. Some of Mill's commentators have recognised the role and importance of this core concept which is an application of its initial exposure by Mill in his *System of Logic* (1843), especially in that part known as *On the Logic of the Moral Sciences* where Mill reveals his concept of ethology which is the science not simply of character but more importantly of the *formation of* character and the development of what Mill calls 'ideal nobleness of character' (Mill 1965, 37–53, 148; Magid 1965). We think that *On Liberty* was intended to overhaul conventional notions of individual and social liberty, inspired in part by the exemplary cultural critiques performed by Socrates and later by Rousseau—both of whom relied on schemes of human development using neglected concepts of individual excellence and civic virtue.

On Liberty is an anatomy of competing models of excellence in the development of both individual and social character. Why then did Mill not simply state the case for the reformed model of liberal virtues he thought modern democracy needed? Mill's first chapter quickly gets to the topic of 'the tyranny of the majority' as the latest threat to political liberty (see e.g. Mill 2015, 47–48). We think that it is this term which helps explain Mill's careful strategy in the lengthy presentation of this work. Mill does not disguise the importance of this new form of 'social tyranny' or 'tyranny of the prevailing opinion and feeling' which he sees as dominating popular government. He notes how powerfully this new system of authority stifles individuality of character and states that this work will try to uncover limits to this power of 'interference' (Mill 2015, 48). We suggest that Mill would have understood that two things will be required to resist this 'interference': resistant individuality of a type illustrated by Socrates or Rousseau; and a moderate public willing at the very least to restrain its policing of dissent and at the very best to promote (i.e., interfere beneficially) civic virtues of reformed liberality. *On Liberty* is Mill's demonstration of how this systemic political reform can be achieved.

Mill's performance as a writer becomes the focus for our bridge-building to help new readers understand this work. *On Liberty* and *Utilitarianism* each comprise five chapters. Both works frame Mill's decade of intensive political activity leading to his election to Parliament. We know how much Mill valued literature and we have seen many examples of his appreciation of the literary character of many of his own works written as public commentary: consider, for example, his pair of essays on the cold prose of Bentham and the warm poetry of Coleridge (Mill 1963, 77–172; 1967). Our supposition is that the two later essays contain five chapters because they are somehow following dramatic practice so evident, for example, in the many five-act plays of dramatists like Shakespeare. Why would Mill 'compose' two essays comprising five chapters? One credible answer is that he saw his task as 'dramatising' changing relationships in the interests and institutions associated with liberty and utility. His five chapters in *On Liberty* trace Mill's movement to reform many of the relationships between citizens and their state at that time in Britain. Over five quite different chapters, Mill performs two important tasks: first he *uncoils* individuals from the power of the state to free them up for greater autonomy; and second, he *recoils* individuals back into a reshaped civil society with a new mission to promote a political culture suitable to the goal of a liberal democracy envisaged by the reformist Mill. Each of the five chapters allows readers to see liberty from a particular perspective, so that when we reach the end of the last chapter we have, following Mill's careful presentation of his reform of orthodox political doctrine, renegotiated relationships between individuals and the state.

Why would Mill 'dramatise' rather than more directly address or orate his reformist political theory? We think that Mill's turn to active political participation was a challenge to 'the tyranny of the majority' and that he would have known that he had no unique skill in tyrannicide suitable for overcoming this prevailing form of popular political power. Mill's brand of reformism was not about new structures of government but about new styles of public thinking, in the hope of promoting a new style of public culture. Thus, Mill needed a strategy to help him establish a workable minority to counter or at least moderate the ruling majority. A brief speech from an unconventional non-politician would hardly do the trick. But a longer 'play of words' written about competing concepts of liberty—soon followed by another 'play of words' about competing concepts of public utility—might get things moving in the direction Mill required. So indeed the two works appeared, each adopting the standard five-chapter mode of presentation.

Mill's strategy in *On Liberty* walks readers through related pathways of individuality and sociality. Each chapter has the two components of liberty interrelated—sometimes closely, often at a distance. Each chapter 'rescripts' relationships between individuals and the state. Two tales of 'rescripting' occur in each chapter of *On Liberty*: in one tale, Mill uncoils individuals from the power of the state in order to lessen the extent of state interference with citizens; and in the other tale, Mill recoils citizens into a reformed version of civil society. Some political experienced readers of Mill's work have celebrated the first tale as primary, often claiming that 'what Mill really meant' is that individuals should be, as far as possible, non-conformists pursuing their own good in their own way, so long as they do no harm to others. These disciples of individualism relish what Mill has to say in the final chapter about the evils of big government, of the deep perils of the 'pedantocracy', and of the dangers of the state which dwarfs citizens into 'small men' (Mill 2015, 148–153).

But these readers discount the other tale which is Mill's recovery of an alternative sense of 'character' which assumes very important political roles when assembled with other virtuous characters in Mill's reformed version of civil society. Mill's model of 'originality' is not confined to those who prefer to remain isolated and alone, or even to those who gather quietly on the edges of civil society to entertain themselves with risk-free activities: true 'originality' becomes an example of 'genius' which can turn around the 'collective mediocrity' of the civic majority. Mill's second tale is about the cultivation (through such works as *On Liberty*) of 'higher eminences' whose 'well-being' outshines 'commonplace humanity': the Athenian leader Pericles is one example cited by Mill who illustrates how a civic culture of 'perfecting and beautifying' citizens can transform a stale democracy into a liberal democracy. The type of reformed regime Mill has in mind promotes an 'intellectually active people' who lead quite differently to 'the tyranny of the majority' precisely because they lead through a new process with a distinctive 'morality of public discussion' based on Socratic virtues of deep listening.

Recovering Character

Mill's detailed plan of argument takes five steps, one with each chapter. This plan involves reformulating liberal progressivism on two fronts: first, by weakening conservative opposition to the advance of liberalism; and second, by weakening liberalism's own opposition to Mill's transformation of individuality into his higher model of character associated with his recovery of nobility and virtue first classical articulated by Plato and Aristotle. Mill is performing politically, by which we mean that he is doing what he can to promote the cause he regards as most important for practical political improvement. But Mill's style of politics has a decidedly persuasive core in that he is not only opposing his enemies but also trying to grow the size of his movement of friends. Knowing that there is little he can do to persuade many conservatives to switch to his side of politics, Mill concentrates on using his rhetorical skills to persuade many of his liberal friends to elevate their conventional utilitarian scheme of majoritarian benefits into something closer to a civic cultivation of nobility and virtue: this strategy of bold persuasion begins in earnest in *On Liberty* and takes full flight in the capstone to Mill's reformulation of progressivism in *Utilitarianism* two years later, which is Mill's equally valuable companion 'essay' (Uhr 2015, 83–102).

It is worth noting some of Mill's careful writing through the example of his opening chapter. This chapter examines a subject which is identified as 'the principal question in human affairs': which is, what rules apply to protect individuals from legal and social control. Unchecked, these controls can develop through 'the magical influence of custom' into the tyranny of the majority (Mill 2015, 49). The role of this initial chapter is to dismantle the power of existing authority to stamp their mark on reformers like Mill. The rhetoric is indirect in that the chapter is a moving statement about the right to autonomy of 'individuals' generally, so long as they do not harm themselves or others. Mill concedes that autonomy is far from complete as a moral claim: society may indeed compel individuals to cease their 'inaction' and begin to help others as an important way of repaying society for the protection it provides to all. But society may not morally conform individuals who prefer to think and act on their own, over and above their routine assistance to others as expected here. The rhetorical exercise in this chapter is to carve out space for an individual like Mill to begin to defend his campaign to reform liberty of thought and action which he does in *On Liberty* and those works which follow it. This introductory chapter is not a generic defence of any or all autonomous individuals but a specific preparation for one particular type of individual modelled on Mill.

This chapter takes aim at the moral logic of majorities, in part by noting that every society has a ruling power which establishes, usually through its prevailing class interests, who counts and who misses out as being part of the majority. Mill's point is that in his own society there is no agreed standard and 'no recognised principle' to limit social or legal interference other than 'personal preferences'. Mill emphatically mentions his own personal preference when he states 'that it seems to me' that British public policy has nothing but preferentialism to guide it when judging whether disputed individual conduct should or should not be regulated. Mill then proposes his own standard which is that 'the only purpose' for such compulsory regulation is 'to prevent harm to others' (Mill 2015, 52–53). The strong implication is external regulation of individuals 'own good' may only happen to prevent harm either to the actor or those likely to be harmed by his action.

Of course, harms do happen. Followers of 'the other Mill' who allegedly represents sociality readily quote many sections of *On Liberty* which emphasise the many circumstances when the threat of harm legitimises regulatory interference. Other followers also note the many sections where the text supports the non-compulsory forms of interference—such as social disapproval—over those whose 'own good' appears ill-informed or wasteful. Still other followers note those sections of the text supporting compulsory interference to goad individuals out of the vice Mill calls 'inaction' so that they will do things 'for the benefit of others' (Mill 2015, 53–54, 96–101, 114–120, 132–136).

Mill knew that he was not the only reformer seeking political attention. We note that the third or central chapter begins and ends with critiques of other 'reformers' who might be promoting a kind of public utility but they are weakening the liberal virtues Mill is hoping to recover and promote. Mill identifies his opponents in what appear to be glowing terms as part of a 'movement' committed to 'philanthropy'. In ways that quietly preview the deeper criticism of *Utilitarianism*, Mill takes aim at the social progressives of his own time by using chilling language: Mill claims that his philanthropic opponents favour 'a thing of small dimensions', so that they are cultivating a society that is in the largest sense a 'collective' yet its components are 'individually small' (Mill 2015, 110). Later Mill claims that his opponents are producing 'small men' (Mill 2015, 153). The issue is mediocrity and Mill's response is his agenda of virtue and nobility which will recover a deeper model of human 'well-being' which can reform orthodox programmes of social improvement.

Conclusion

Mill knew that his rhetoric in *On Liberty* would cause offence. The logic of the work helped him believe that this rhetoric would not cause harm which would entitle those harmed to hold him to account. But offence is a lesser problem: Mill would not be surprised that *On Liberty* has offended many political conservatives whose respect for traditional authority makes them uncomfortable with the theme of individuality celebrated in this work; nor would he be surprised that *On Liberty* has offended many liberals whose respect for majoritarian public utility puts them at a distance from Mill's insistent defence of the cultivation of excellence and the pursuit of individual and civic virtue. Mill advocates or at least anticipates a revised form of utilitarianism based on 'utility in the largest sense' (Mill 2015, 54). Mill's deepest ambition was to perform a challenging political feat which was to persuade a significant number of former conservatives and liberals to become progressives in the new mould being articulated in works like *On Liberty* and, soon to follow, *Utilitarianism*.

New students of Mill will know that he is often regarded as a champion of minorities and that *On Liberty* is often read as defence of minorities and possibly as a defence of socially non-conformist libertarianism. There is something of the truth in these claims. Yet the real minority group being targeted by Mill's *On Liberty* is women and those who want to champion the rights of women. The rhetoric of *On Liberty* is designed to assemble a new force of progressives with interests in minority rights, starting with women and their feminist friends who want to include women in political affairs, but reaching substantially beyond this group to those interested more generally in promoting the rights of the missing or unnoticed minority of virtuous characters who can generate a new sense of nobility into democratic politics. This remarkable element of *democratic elitism* evident in Mill's political rhetoric has attracted some close scholarly attention but little of it has interpreted *On Liberty* as the start of Mill's decade of active political performance. Mill entered the House of Commons as the advocate of neglected minorities in whose interest he was to propose such practical reforms as proportional representation to better represent the voices of virtues so often neglected in modern democratic politics.

References

Alexander, Edward. 1967. Introduction. *J. S. Mill Literary Essays*. New York: Bobbs-Merrill.

Bailey, Andrew. 2012. *The Broadview Anthology of Social and Political Thought: Essential Readings*, ed. Andrew Bailey et al. Toronto: Broadview Press.

Himmelfarb, Gertrude. 1963. Introduction. In *Essays on Politics and Culture*, ed. G. Himmelfarb. New York: Anchor Books.

Himmelfarb, Gertrude. 1985. Introduction. In *On Liberty*, ed. G. Himmelfarb. London: Penguin Books.

Himmelfarb, Gertrude. 2006. *The Moral Imagination*. Chicago: Ivan R Dee Books.

Magid, Henry M. 1965. Introduction. In *On the Logic of the Moral Sciences*, ed. H.M. Magid. Indianapolis: Bobs-Merrill Library of Liberal Arts.

Mill, J.S. 1963. *Essays on Politics and Culture*, edited with an Introduction by Gertrude Himmelfarb. New York: Anchor Books.

Mill, J.S. 1965. *On the Logic of the Moral Sciences*, edited with an Introduction by Henry M. Magid. Indianapolis: Bobs-Merrill Liberal of Liberal Arts.

Mill, J.S. 1967. *Mill on Bentham and Coleridge*, Introduction by F.R. Leavis. London: Chatto and Windus.

Mill, J.S. 1991a. *Autobiography*, edited with an Introduction by Jack Stillinger. Oxford: Oxford University Press.
Mill, J.S. 1991b. *On Liberty and Other Essays*, edited with an Introduction by John Gray. Oxford: Oxford University Press.
Mill, J.S. 2015. *On Liberty*, ed. Leonard Kahn. Toronto: Broadview Press.
Uhr, John. 2015. *Prudential Public Leadership*. London: Palgrave.

CHAPTER 6

Reading Nietzsche's *On the Genealogy of Morals*

Performing as an Artist

Abstract The fifth lesson comes from Nietzsche. *On the Genealogy of Morals* is a complicated and dense work. But is the one intended by Nietzsche to re-educate readers into something we now call postmodernism. Nietzsche's strategy is to confront readers with a challenge, which is to recover their greatness by abandoning or destroying egalitarian morality, and preparing for the return of a culture of human greatness.

Keywords Master morality · Slave morality · Religion · Priests · Artists

To perform 'as an artist' means to use artistic powers to enrich our understanding of human greatness. Nietzsche's interest in the recovery of greatness in modern culture urges him to specify the qualities of greatness missing because of the dominance of egalitarian morality in the modern West. The best specifications of moral alternatives come from artists (writers, musicians, painters) with the power to reshape our understanding of culture, including what we now call political culture. Performing as an artist here means destroying and rewriting culture with the aim of cultivating the kinds of human greatness, including moral greatness, celebrated by Nietzsche.

The original version of this chapter was revised: Belated author correction has been corrected. The erratum to this chapter is available at https://doi.org/10.1007/978-981-10-7998-6_8

© The Author(s) 2018
J. Uhr, *Performing Political Theory*,
https://doi.org/10.1007/978-981-10-7998-6_6

85

As a student of political theory, Nietzsche might have considered other types of performance to transform conventional politics: a common type we find in his works is 'the founder' performing the roles celebrated by Machiavelli in *The Prince*. In important ways, Nietzsche is credited as a founder of what we call 'postmodernism', meaning the way of life going beyond the liberal-individualist modernism promoted by the Enlightenment. Nietzsche's 'postmodernism' signals the call to arms for artists who are expected to manage the transition from the modern West towards 'postmodernism'—and what Nietzsche thought of as the revival of 'great politics'. Nietzsche moves in the shadow of Machiavelli, using his *Genealogy of Morals* to propose a new type of artistic founder who will reshape the political culture of modern Europe. Nietzsche's founder-artist is a cultural architect, acting as an artist at large rather than as a regulatory ruler: an artist who can reconfigure the political horizon and reconstruct the political culture to prompt the development of a new type of human greatness.

Our working textbook includes Nietzsche's *On the Genealogy of Morals* which we have come to see as a problem text when teaching the history of modern political thought. Genealogical methods of social inquiry have flourished since Nietzsche demonstrated their promising relevance (Bergoffen 1983; Lampert 1993, 1–13, 443–446; Owen 2008, 142–145). The *Genealogy* is claimed to be 'the most widely discussed of Nietzsche's books' (Reginster 1996, 457). Yet critics of this influential theorist claim that he used his innovative method quite loosely, as a thinker who 'names no names, dates no events, and shows scant concern for details, variations, and anomalies', making his genealogy an example of 'inspired guesswork, suggestive speculation, or a likely tale' (Berkowitz 1995, 68–69). It is no surprise then that young university students with an interest in the study of politics often do not know what to make of Nietzsche generally, and they find this particular text and 'the great debates' it provokes too distant from their own experience of everyday politics (Roochnik 2016, 114–125).

The editors of the Broadview Anthology alert new readers when they note that Nietzsche writes this work with many aphorisms and short entries, making him one 'of the few great stylists among philosophers' who uses a wide range of literary devices 'designed to provoke the reader': but this 'doesn't make for easy reading' (Bailey 2012, 746). Not for nothing does Nietzsche put Mill as on his list of 'impossible people' with his impossibly 'offensive lucidity' (Nietzsche 2007, 48). How then do we use our bridge-building powers in this demanding case? The answer is hard to formulate because this puzzling text seems more about 'morality' than 'politics' and students might well think that, having studied Machiavelli to see how widely separated morality and politics can be, it goes against this grain of modernity to turn away from politics as Machiavelli celebrated it and towards morality as Nietzsche examines it (Lampert 1993, 324–330).

In fact, this link to Machiavelli is exactly the case we make when inviting students to read Nietzsche. The agenda of modernity as devised by Machiavelli's *The Prince* warns us against expecting too much morality in politics. The allure of Nietzsche is that morality returns as primary in a text about the origins and historical 'genius' of 'morality'. For Machiavelli, morality makes sense when seen through the eyes of political *virtu* as revealed in *The Prince*. For Nietzsche, politics makes sense when seen through the eyes of the 'master morality' as this is revealed in *On the Genealogy of Morals*. The comparison is broadly between modernity as understood by Machiavelli and what we now call postmodernism as framed by Nietzsche in works of such dazzling brilliance as this fascinating work. Nietzsche's sustained interest in philosophers as the most interesting models of cultivated humanity has been seen not simply as apolitical but antipolitical (Zuckert 1983, 49, 70–71).

A more conventional approach to bridge-building would be to see Nietzsche as illustrating one of three core political perspectives in contemporary times. Mill is often used to illustrate the political centre or conventional mainstream of liberal democracy; Marx is just as often used to illustrate the perspective of the left in contemporary politics; and so too Nietzsche can be used to illustrate the perspective of the right in contemporary politics. We tend to avoid this approach because it assumes that Nietzsche 'caused' or 'shaped' right-wing politics from extreme examples like that of the Nazi regime to later examples of protectionist populism. Our approach is to try to see Nietzsche more on his own terms, so that we and our students can make some distinctions between his high-grade politics of 'master morality' and the low-grade politics of contemporary right-wing movements. Sure enough, there is no limiting the many ways that later right-wing groups can appropriate some of Nietzsche's thoughts, especially those relating to the errors of equality and the need for strong leadership; nor is there much that can be done to slow down the transfer of some of Nietzsche's thoughts to later left-wing groups, especially those thoughts relating to the staleness of democratic culture and art. But our approach is to help students see Nietzsche as a formative voice of postmodernism with its re-evaluation of the mainstream morality of liberal modernity treasured by such central political figures as John Stuart Mill, who is described by Nietzsche as one of the 'mediocre minds' and 'mediocre spirits' and 'mediocre Englishmen' he had encountered—a custodian of 'the plebeianism of modern ideas' (*Beyond Good and Evil*, section 253 in Nietzsche 1966, 191–192).

THE PREFACE

Nietzsche's subtitle for *On the Genealogy of Morals* is 'a polemic'. This is the first hint we have of the curiously political character of this work. Part of the polemic is directed at the rule of modern ideas which is the theme of *Beyond Good and Evil* as highlighted in the important Preface to this work (Nietzsche 1989, 15–23; Detwiler 1990, 3, 27–31). Our initial steps towards Nietzsche's thinking begin with the first pages of his writing: with the eight sections of the Preface. This preliminary part of the work reveals that Nietzsche is about to show how we moderns, who pride ourselves on being 'men of knowledge', really know very little about 'the *origin* of our moral prejudices' which is the precise subject 'of this polemic' (Nietzsche 1989, 15). Nietzsche speaks as 'a philosopher' (and later as 'a psychologist') interested in what he terms 'free spirits': a type of human being to emerge as a politically important feature of this work. This type will be contrasted with prevailing human types such as the liberal free thinkers ('the genuinely *English* type') associated with intellectual leaders like John Stuart Mill. Nietzsche asks his readers to question our sources of knowledge to learn how we devised 'these value judgments' about the nature of good and evil (Lampert 1993, 326).

Taking close note of the high priority we moderns give to the value of 'pity', Nietzsche critically evaluates modern European culture as drenched so much in this value that it has become not only preoccupied with 'nothingness' but a captive of '*nihilism*' (Nietzsche 1989, 19). Inviting his readers to join him as he examines 'the value of these "values"', Nietzsche formulates his thesis that the modern morality of pity has become 'the danger of dangers' in the specific sense that pity has extinguished '*the highest power and splendour*' open to humanity. Nietzsche presents himself as searching for help so that we can escape from nihilism. The thinker acts as a writer who is engaged in community-formation in a much deeper sense that we found Mill doing in *On Liberty*. Nietzsche can be seen as a political actor forming his readers into a political movement against the despondent nihilism he sees afflicting modern democracy, causing 'this nausea, this weariness' (Nietzsche 1989, 121). Students look more closely at Nietzsche when they see him inviting them to be 'comrades' and to share in his oddly attractive 'cheerfulness'—at the prospect of his entertaining 'comedy'—which contrasts so much with 'the pessimism and weariness' of modern moralists and intellects (Nietzsche 1989, 21–22; Zuckert 1983, 52).

The Preface ends with Nietzsche's challenging words about his style of writing. He admits that he is 'not easy to penetrate' and that one of his literary devices is the aphorism which he claims have to be 'deciphered', with an example of this type of close reading 'as an *art*' given in the third of the three essays comprising *On the Genealogy of Morals*. This solid hint about what Nietzsche calls 'his method' allows us to invite students to see where Nietzsche wants to move his audience: 'my *unknown* friends' (Nietzsche 1989, 161). We are not revising or reconstructing the author to make him palatable to novice palates; instead, we are helping students begin to see the author as performing a political task as he guides us through the confusing pathways of this curious work about the formation of 'free spirits' who will soon be invited to take on demanding political roles—as political artists shaping the world of postmodernism.

We also highlight the important 'note' at the end of the first essay where Nietzsche clarifies his relationship as an author to his readers and highlights the thesis of 'this treatise' as determining the order of rank among values (Nietzsche 1989, 55–56). In fact, Nietzsche has several ways of drawing attention to the writer–reader relationship which is worth bringing to the attention of new students. At some points, he writes directly to 'you', asking if it is true that 'you do not comprehend this' (Nietzsche 1989, 34). At other points, he writes like a dramatist, using imagined dialogue from 'Mr Rash and Curious' who is invited to speak: 'now I am the one who is listening', he says, as he recites nearly three pages of imagined speech by one who is asked to 'say what you see' (Nietzsche 1989, 46–48). Nietzsche also refers to 'my readers' in certain passages where he indicates how they can relate this work to other works, like *Beyond Good and Evil* (Nietzsche 1989, 54–55). For good reasons, critics see Nietzsche as very interested in 'the practical problem of persuasion' where opponents' theories can be adapted and reframed as credible weapons against them—and later discarded (Reginster 1996, 459).

Essay Three

Taking Nietzsche at his word, we guide students to this third essay (Nietzsche 1989, 97–163). Here we find an opening aphorism from one of Nietzsche's other works, *Thus Spoke Zarathrustra*, with echoes of words first heard by students when reading Chap. 25 of *The Prince*: 'wisdom is a woman and always loves only a warrior' (Nietzsche 1989, 97). The Preface states that this third essay models 'exegesis' in that the essay as a whole is a commentary on this aphorism. How do we help students make their way through the 28 sections occupying 60 pages—especially when this third essay is not included in the Broadview Anthology we generally use (Bailey 2012, 749–770)? The essay is entitled: 'What is the meaning of ascetic ideals?' (Nietzsche 1989, 97). The essay-commentary begins by noting how widely shared is the ascetic ideal, explained soon after to mean the unstable equilibrium between higher and lower or between ascetic and sensual where the ascetic ideal restrains ever-present sensuality. The composer Wagner is made the disconcerting example of an artist only slowly prepared at last to laugh at his earlier ascetic ideals. The second and more promising example is the German philosopher Schopenhauer whose case illustrates the power of the ascetic ideal to free a person from 'his torture' of human sensuality through this 'most powerful activity' which is the 'path to power' through the three 'great slogans' of poverty, humility and chastity. This is what turns a person into a 'free spirit' drawn to what Nietzsche describes as a 'desert': meaning a place for the quiet and unnoticed anonymity of analysis, cultivated by those spirits who prefer 'concealment' (Nietzsche 1989, 106–112; Berkowitz 1995, 90–96).

At the heart of postmodernism is a rejection of the Enlightenment model of rationality and an acceptance of new forms of 'objectivity' where we begin 'to see differently...to *want* to see differently'. The author invites readers to get ready 'to employ a variety of perspectives and affective interpretations' so that we can learn to know more about the origins, and presumably the applications, of morality. Traditional objectivity loses its power as a standard, to be replaced by '*only* a perspective seeing, *only* a perspective "knowing"' (Nietzsche 1989, 118–119). The modern world is already shaped within a range of perspectives, so that the new political order will emerge as a new set of perspectives challenges and replaces those nurturing 'the cultural domain' of modernity. The challenge for Nietzsche is to arouse a spirit to smother what he calls '*ressentiment*' which is his special term to describe prevailing political morality of excessive pity which acts as revenge against enemies of the ethos of modernity (Nietzsche 1989, 121–125; Detwiler 1990, 127–133).

Nietzsche's sense of politics emerges in his use of 'tyranny' to describe the type of effective rule carried out by those shepherding 'the herd';

but it also emerges in his remarkable (and oddly bracketed) paragraph in section 16 of the third essay dealing with 'readers of the kind I need' (Nietzsche 1989, 128–129). Here he states that what the ruling shepherds think of as the 'sickness' of modern man is really nothing but an 'interpretation'. Nietzsche thinks of politics as an *interpretative* activity, with this third essay slowing trying to gather greater public interest in his own interpretation about the need for 'free spirits' who can transform public morality from sickness to health. The medium of this political conflict will not be through elections or systems of representative government but through 'polemics' about culture when that is understood as 'the psychological-moral domain' (Nietzsche 1989, 130). Nietzsche contrasts the use of 'dishonest lies' in modern politics with his alternative 'real lie, a genuine lie, resolute, "honest"' lie—later called a '*will to deception*' (Nietzsche 1989, 137, 153). The function of such honest lies is evident to 'us psychologists' but remains inaccessible to contemporary leaders who see themselves as revengeful against alternative forms of political rule, each democratic shepherd displaying his priest-like craft as an 'artist in guilt feelings': imposing rule as a form of punishment for our sins (Nietzsche 1989, 139–141; Lampert 1993, 342).

Nietzsche asks readers to help him find 'an opposing ideal' to that of the governing ascetic ideal and its close companion 'modern science' which effectively promote among Nietzsche's circle of potential radicals 'the unrest of lack of ideals, the suffering from the lack of any great love' (Nietzsche 1989, 147). Eventually, in section 24, Nietzsche identifies 'the last idealists'—'the honor of our age'—who might provide him with his new army of reformers, capable of becoming genuine 'free spirits' if and when they can lose '*their faith in truth*'. The claim from Nietzsche is that already raised in radical circles: 'nothing is true; everything is permitted' (Nietzsche 1989, 150). His hope is that this battle cry might force these potential free spirits to overthrow their 'renunciation of all interpretation' and their restraining 'will to truth' which is about to be replaced by 'the will to power' which features so prominently in this third essay. The 'will to truth requires a critique' which Nietzsche reckons will cause the collapse of public morality over 'the next two centuries in Europe' (Nietzsche 1989, 148–153, 161; Zuckert 1983, 69–70; Detwiler 1990, 138; Lampert 1993, 437–438). This was written just under a century and a half ago!

It can help new students to see Nietzsche's 'historical method' as something like earlier state of nature theories with their fascinating historical accounts of the transmission into civil society through a social contract which transformed isolated individuals into political communities. The invention of concepts like bad conscience and of guilt are somewhat similar to the invention of natural laws by earlier theorists of the social contract, for whom civil law brings about forms of justice that are absent in the state of nature. Nietzsche follows pioneers like Rousseau who wrote his *Second Discourse* to fight back against the downgrading mediocrity of supposed progress; so too, Nietzsche fights back against the deadening progress of modernity through his own version of what Rousseau had called natural savages. Nietzsche's anthropology of 'prehistory' becomes not only a preview of life before modernity but also what we might call a 'postview' of life after modernity—that is, of 'postmodernism' (see e.g. Nietzsche 1989, 88–89, 92; Zuckert 1983, 50–51, 56–59; Owen 2008, 150–153; Roochnik 2016, 117).

ESSAY ONE

What then about helping students to go back to the beginning and read the first and second essays? The 17 sections in the first essay examine core concepts of good and bad, and good and evil. The 25 sections of the second essay examine a looser configuration of concepts, such as guilt, bad conscience 'and the like' (Nietzsche 1989, 57). The first essay is a slow and measured contrast of modern or 'slave' morality with the ancient or 'master' morality from which it broke away. The focus is primarily on the limits of modern morality, with a restrained revelation of what a profound difference would come if somehow the lost alternative morality were recovered or revived, as it is in greater fullness in the second essay. Thus, the first essay is more diagnostic than the second and the second essay is more therapeutic than the first. Students can benefit when reading Nietzsche if they are prepared to see the probable point of his three-part plan of engagement with his readers. Edited versions which reduce this plan from three to two essays make this hazardous; those which further edit out many parts of these two essays leave readers wondering about the missing art behind the cumbersome presentation; and those versions which also delete the Preface rob readers of Nietzsche's rhetorical performance where he stages the relationships between writer and readers (see e.g. Bailey 2012, 749–770).

The first essay begins with very critical comments about the prevailing wisdom of 'English psychologists' who claim to know so much about the origin of morality (Detwiler 1990, 117–119). Readers receive a lot of help from Nietzsche as he uses this first essay to provide something of a character portrait of conventional wisdom about the origin and development of morality. But he limits his use of evidence of this school to only a few instances where figures like Spencer and Buckle are cited; and he spends far more time in clarifying the dynamic opposition between the lost world of master morality and the priestly ethos driving the modern European culture of slave morality. The English psychologists have value because they illustrate the rise of bland mediocrity as the end-effect of slave morality, possibly unaware not only of the attractive power of the master morality exemplified by classical exponents like the noble warrior Pericles, but also of the religious undercurrent of slave morality exemplified by Jewish and Christian leaders. This first essay works slowly around three sets of ideas: first are the ideas of modern democracy and its political culture of flat equality reducing concepts of nobility and greatness to comfortable well-being for all; second are the driving ideas of slave morality best illustrated by the priest caste with its the sense of deep *ressentiment* against inequalities of master morality; and third are the ideas of master morality cultivated in part by modern leaders like Napoleon who reflect the ancient greatness originally represented by figures like Pericles or even earlier by Homer's legendary hero Achilles (Nietzsche 1989, 54). The purpose of this first essay is to allow readers to distance themselves from the comfort of conventional wisdom and to see what is at stake in Nietzsche's rearticulation of a version of the battle of ideas between the ancients and the moderns.

The sources being relied on by Nietzsche in this first essay are three: those flying the flag of the conventional political culture of deadening conformity so ably managed by 'English psychologists'; those challenging the driving spirit of slave morality through its religious championing of pity for the underdog and revenge against those we might term 'the over-dogs' like Napoleon and Pericles; and the frequently poetic advocates of a system of master morality which promises to retain some important measure of the greatness open to humanity if Nietzsche proves to be correct in his analysis of our plight (Detwiler 1990, 49–50). The first essay presents three field tests which readers can use to get their intellectual bearings. The ambition of the writer is to move readers through the succession of discomfort with 'English' mediocrity to uneasiness with the deeper set of values in slave morality to a final location where readers begin to wonder about the feasibility and potential recovery of something like master morality. Essays two and three move readers more assuredly through the latter stages of this sequence. But this recovery depends very much on the performance experienced by readers as they encounter their way through the complex pathways of the three sets of core ideas in the first essay.

The first essay is an exercise in decomposition, with Nietzsche inviting readers to think themselves out of alignment with their supportive political environment. Part of the style of this performance comes from Nietzsche's reliance on the contrast between the culture of comfort for all and the underlying religious values of supportive pity and vengeful *ressentiment*. The attention to the leadership role of priests is likely to signal a warning to agnostic or atheistic moderns who might dislike being so dependent on the priestly leadership of the type uncovered by Nietzsche. Another part of the performance style crafted by Nietzsche is the longing for human greatness he identifies in the first essay and the daunting image of the warrior ('the blond beast') he uses to mobilise readers' interest in recovering a master morality. Each of these three competing systems of evaluation moves the mind of readers as they struggle through the first essay. Our experience is that it helps to keep these three mind pictures in front of students and to work them through as though they were assembled as thesis–antithesis–synthesis.

The opening picture is that celebrated by 'English psychologists' who complacently assume that morality is all about utility and that bad morality is mostly about 'pride'—which Nietzsche will later suggest we can learn to enjoy. The utility focus turns out to be unenjoyable: it is 'common and plebeian', part of 'the democratic prejudice' at home in the herd instinct growing across contemporary Europe (Nietzsche 1989, 25–28). The second picture emerges as Nietzsche identifies a superior caste in the form of 'the *priestly* caste' performing a 'priestly function' not widely understood in modernity. The Jews are the first 'priestly people' who began the slave revolt in morality, taken over as a morality of love under Christianity: both versions were built on revenge against the supposed nobility of master moralities of inequality. This 'mobized' morality has promoted the interests of 'the common man' and become the close friend of democracy. The slave morality is reactive: it is defined by its opposition to 'the noble mode of evaluation' which is, instead, one of the initiatives. The end result is the cultivation of the bland, evident in such features as the 'tame man' pictured by Nietzsche; and again the 'mediocre and insipid man'; and more generally, the 'diminution and levelling of

European man'; and even finally, 'the lowering, the abasement, the levelling and the decline and twilight of mankind' (Nietzsche 1989, 31–37, 43–44, 54).

The third picture is far from finished in this second essay. It is the picture of nobility rather than equality, of higher rather than lower ranks. The 'good' comes from warriors and we see how 'the warrior caste' can retake their former place seized by the priestly caste. Nietzsche identifies the importance of 'Greek nobility' and uses as one of his primary examples, Pericles (Nietzsche 1989, 28–31, 37, 41). The claim is that grand leaders like Pericles activated an 'ancient nobler aristocratic mode of evaluation' and that their role today remains as preferred examples of the 'higher man' Nietzsche invites his readers to search for. The nature of this type of unconventional leader becomes clouded when we see Nietzsche lauding the lost type with the language of 'blond beasts' or 'beasts of prey' who stand out as warriors in command of a master morality. Politically, the case is not only in terms of named individuals but also in terms of named polities, such as the defence of Rome against the modernising spirit of Judea (Nietzsche 1989, 38, 40–43, 52–54).

Perhaps the largest theme likely to win student interest is the imbalance between good and bad and good and evil. Nietzsche uses the whole of this first essay to carry through his earlier case in *Beyond Good and Evil* that 'evil' is an artefact of slave morality capable of holding us back from recovering the lost nobility of master morality. Defining good as a response to 'evil' is an invention of the religious spirit of modernity which fears that the morality of grandeur is a threat to what we love most in humanity, which is our care for equality and the morality of pity we orchestrate around it. The alternative is another interpretation of the good which illustrates an alternative interpretation of humanity: this alternative is hierarchical rather than democratic, noble rather than plebeian, and will only again come clearly into sight when we follow Nietzsche's advice and cultivate 'free spirits' who can see 'beyond good and evil' and move us back, as it were, before the spread of the Old and New Testaments, so that we can recover 'the origins' of morality and the politics of greatness it might inspire (Nietzsche 1989, 40, 44, 52).

Essay Two

Nietzsche opens the second essay with a contrast between promise-keeping and something he calls 'forgetfulness'. The whole essay is really about the positive qualities of this activity of 'forgetfulness'. Nietzsche is coaching his readers in a new form of 'forgetfulness' intended to move us away from our adherence to the conventional wisdom of keeping our promises, towards space where we can forget about the restrictive cultural norms of modern well-being. This strange work of decomposition will strip us of our prevailing morality-memory in the hope that we reverse the process of *ressentiment* and erase our sense of revenge we have been taught to hold against the premodern prospect of masterfulness.

This essay is an exploration of cultural anthropology showing the evolution of what Nietzsche terms 'a morality of mores' around habits of responsible calculation praised as the free will expected of emancipated human beings. The point for Nietzsche is that this modern model of mastery pales in comparison with the real alternative of master morality being slowly recovered in this essay. The early sections provide a portrait of modern masterfulness which starts to fade and lose its vitality as we focus in on the specific forms of moral responsibility it develops. The conscience seems to be the governor of this process but Nietzsche suggests that the conscience is a regulative device to punish misconduct more than an inspiration device to promote good conduct. The conscience draws on concepts of guilt to steer individuals away from bad conduct, with a doctrine of 'evil' constructed to dramatise the threatened nature of the good.

Nietzsche's unconventional account of the indebtedness of bad conduct helps him turn the focus to punishment and more importantly the 'severity, cruelty, and pain' caused by those undergoing punishment (Nietzsche 1989, 64). The history of morality shows how man has become 'ashamed' of that early cruelty and so promoted a 'morbid softening and moralization' hiding 'this joy in cruelty': joy here referring to the public theatre recollected by Nietzsche in his evocation of 'prehistory' and its primitive concepts of community-indebted punishment. Modern culture removes itself from the earlier culture of cruelty with a 'semiotically concentrated' process of redefinition with confusing concepts of punishment using 'utilities of all kinds' (Nietzsche 1989, 65–72, 80–81).

At a certain point, Nietzsche contrasts the conventional 'English' wisdom about the process of historical adaptation with a better account of what drives history, which is the 'will to power' so misunderstood by modern people who prefer the 'democratic idiosyncracy' labelled by Nietzsche as 'the *modern misarchism*' or hatred of rule (Nietzsche 1989, 76–79). Contrary to social contract theorists, Nietzsche uses the term 'state' to introduce the role of state rulers who have imposed the state apparatus through their conquests. The concept of 'master' relates to the capacity to exercise 'command', with Nietzsche sketching a wide range of commanding capacities: those who can impose 'forms' carry out the power of command, and this definitely includes something like the artistic form of *On the Genealogy of Morals*. New students of Nietzsche find it difficult to make easy sense of the commanding 'will to power' exercised through 'their hammer blows and artists' violence' (Nietzsche 1989, 86–87; Detwiler 1990, 101–102, 110; Lampert 1993, 331–332).

It seems that political and artistic power are related, as we learn from the discussion of 'those artists of violence and organizers who build states'. The uneasiness of students grows as they ponder the place of 'artists' cruelty' when seized by 'delight' to impose 'form' on material. Our explanation is that students can begin by thinking of Nietzsche's own 'delight' as he imposed the cruelty of his *Genealogy* on modern democratic culture. The discordant language of 'illness' starts to make some sense when we ask students to consider Nietzsche's careful description of 'pregnancy' as an illness—and the even more careful description of the 'man of the future' (yet to be born) as 'this Antichrist and antinihilist' (Nietzsche 1989, 87–88, 96).

Conclusion

The review of our approach to Nietzsche's *On the Genealogy of Morals* has emphasised how tentative and cautious we are in building a bridge between students and this disorienting work of high theory. Admittedly, the work can be read as 'an illustrative myth or poem' (Berkowitz 1995, 70). Characteristically, Nietzsche's method as a political thinker includes frequent attention to his role as a writer and the vast distance so many readers will find between themselves and his works. As academic teachers, the best we can do is to bridge-build across that expansive distance so that students can begin to take a closer personal stake in how they read this masterful writer and how they can start to reconstruct his elusive political theory (Roochnik 2016, 120–124).

Students new to Nietzsche might benefit from knowing that *On the Genealogy of Morals* was intended as a supplement to the earlier work *Beyond Good and Evil*—explicitly referred to on a number of times (see e.g. Nietzsche 1989, 55, 66). Teachers might think that it would then help to begin by reading that earlier work. Other commentators look to later works such as *Ecce Homo* with its reflections on earlier works like *On the Genealogy of Morals*. The complication is that all these works are very deep encounters with the cultural sources of humanity and our experience is that new students are likely to be puzzled and confused by Nietzsche's cultural anthropology used 'to show how man has become man, and how he may become more than man' (Dannhauser 1974, 189). The brief entry on this work in *Ecce Homo* notes that it is 'a polemic' which implies that is it not intended to be the last word from this thinker on this topic, and possibly that the work is deliberately provocative as well as illustrating 'preliminary studies' towards 'a revaluation of all values' (Nietzsche 1989, 313).

Nietzsche admits in *Ecce Homo* that the essays of the *Genealogy* are 'uncannier than anything else written so far', with the work containing 'perfectly gruesome denotations'. Students here see the author making remarkably succinct summaries of each of the three essays. We learn that the first essay reveals that 'the spirit of *ressentiment*' is not only reactive but also a 'great rebellion against the domination of *noble* values'. Whatever replaces the so-called nobility of master morality has its own edge which Nietzsche calls 'cruelty': a very daring way of describing the type of egalitarianism and anti-elitism students can begin to appreciate when studying the political culture of modern democracy (Nietzsche 1989, 312–313).

References

Bailey, Andrew, et al. (eds.). 2012. *The Broadview Anthology of Social and Political Thought: Essential Readings*. Toronto: Broadview Press.

Bergoffen, Debra A. 1983. Why a Genealogy of Morals? *Man and World* 16: 129–138.

Berkowitz, Peter. 1995. *Nietzsche: The Ethics of an Immoralist*. Cambridge: Harvard University Press.

Dannhauser, Werner. 1974. *Nietzsche's View of Socrates*. Ithaca: Cornell University Press.
Detwiler, Bruce. 1990. *Nietzsche and the Politics of Aristocratic Radicalism*. Chicago: University of Chicago Press.
Lampert, Laurence. 1993. *Nietzsche and Modern Times*. New Haven: Yale University Press.
Nietzsche, Friedrich. 1966. *Beyond Good and Evil*. Translated with Commentary by Walter Kaufmann. New York: Vintage Books.
Nietzsche, Friedrich. 1989. *On the Genealogy of Morals* and *Ecce Homo*, edited with Commentary by Walter Kaufmann. New York: Vintage Books.
Nietzsche, Friedrich. 2007. *Twilight of the Idols*. Translated by Antony Ludovici with an Introduction by Ray Furness. Ware, Herdfordshire: Wordsworth Editions.
Owen, David. 2008. Nietzsche's Genealogy Revisited. *Journal of Nietzsche Studies* (35/36): 141–154.
Reginster, Bernard. 1996. Review of R. Schacht, 'Nietzsche, Genealogy, Morality'. *Ethics* 106 (2): 457–459.
Roochnik, David. 2016. *Thinking Philosophically: An Introduction to the Great Debates*. Oxford: Wiley Blackwell.
Zuckert, Catherine. 1983. Nietzsche on the Origin and Development of the Distinctively Human. *Polity* 16 (1): 48–71.

CHAPTER 7

Conclusion: Reading Collingwood

Performing as an Interpreter

Abstract The sixth and final lesson comes from recent academic studies of textual interpretation. R. G. Collingwood makes the first step in his generally ignored 1933 work on philosophical method. Leo Strauss takes the second step with his punishing critique of Collingwood's theories of interpretation. The third step is taken by Claude Lefort whose theories of writing and reading rehabilitate Strauss as the philosopher-interpreter necessary for those wanting to understand the history of modern political theory.

Keywords Collingwood · Strauss · Lefort · Interpretation · Criticism Commentary · Reading

Performing Political Theory has made a case that pedagogy is part of the world of political theory performance. I have argued that academic teachers of political theory can help new students learn much about the historical development of modern political theory by clarifying the ways that great thinkers about political theory were often great writers interested in political education. My case has been that the type of great political theorists examined in the cases studies in this book—Machiavelli, Mill and Nietzsche—have also been great educators; their performance

---

The original version of this chapter was revised: Belated author correction has been corrected. The erratum to this chapter is available at
https://doi.org/10.1007/978-981-10-7998-6_8

© The Author(s) 2018
J. Uhr, *Performing Political Theory*,
https://doi.org/10.1007/978-981-10-7998-6_7

as political theorists include very significant performance as educational writers, where their writing becomes a course of education for those readers prepared to take on this demanding type of unconventional reading.

Academic teachers are also performing a role in political theory. They are bridge-builders trying to bring students closer to those political theorists who have shaped the many ways we look at politics in the contemporary world. I have devised a model of this academic bridge-building drawn from the theory of 'criticism' developed by Lord Shaftesbury who formulated a distinctive relationship between writers and readers around what he thought of as the related performances of critical writing and critical reading—where writers and readers together promote a civic culture of liberal learning. The concluding themes examined in this final chapter are the instruments of interpretation academic teachers offer to students reading great works of writing in political theory. It seems that here too there are performative puzzles: debates over competing schemes of textual interpretation tend to show that reading great writings requires special kinds of intellectual performance as readers reconstruct or reconfigure or recalibrate elements left incomplete or disorganised by writers who knew when enough had already been said to convey their discernible doctrines. Each of the books I have examined by Machiavelli, Mill and Nietzsche were intentionally incomplete: the writers left work for their readers to perform as they learnt how to think and act politically.

Performing as an interpreter is one way of describing the role of academic teachers as they use their pedagogical skills to help students learn more about interpretative readings of great writings in political theory. What can readers learn about the performance writers require of them? Academic teachers can act as critics by showing new readers some of the ways that old writers framed interpretative performance. This chapter tells one story in this tale by walking readers back from the critical theory of Claude Lefort as he invites us to consider the classical interpretative theory of Leo Strauss who in turn invites us to consider the modern interpretative theory of R. G. Collingwood. All these scholars are exemplary academic teachers of political theory whose research investigates the dramatic performance of textual interpretation, with much that can strengthen contemporary pedagogy.

In this concluding chapter, I want to recover a version of the art of writing which corresponds to Shaftesbury's critical art of reading, which I have used as a working model of the style of bridge-building suitable for contemporary academic teachers of the history of modern political thought. This convenient correspondence is from English philosopher R. G. Collingwood's surprisingly neglected *An Essay on Philosophical Method* first published in 1933 (Collingwood 2008). Collingwood's interest in literary 'method' is unusual in philosophical studies, so we can anticipate special value from a close reading of his penultimate chapter on 'philosophy as a branch of literature' (Collingwood 2008, 199–220). This unusual account of the literary qualities of philosophy—promoted by Henze in his study of 'the style of philosophy'—helps me round out my analysis of critical pedagogy as a theme of writing and reading political theory (Henze 1980, 420).

The Relevance of Collingwood

This chapter examines methods for interpreting texts in political theory. The name of English philosopher R. G. Collingwood (1889–1943) appears in the chapter title, yet this name has so far made only one very brief appearance in this book—as a passing reference in Chapter 2. Although Collingwood is the author of a number of works of political theory, few of these find their way into standard courses on the history of modern political theory. One of his last works was *The New Leviathan* with a title referring back to Thomas Hobbes' famous work in English political theory, the *Leviathan*. In recent years, some 19 of his essays in political philosophy have been collected and republished, giving us one important indication of his persistent interest in political practice and also political theory (Collingwood 1989). Students of political theory might well include Collingwood in a study of twentieth-century thinking about the concept of the political. Certainly, students of theories of idealism include Collingwood in their studies of British attempts to devise idealist alternatives to mainstream models of political realism (Boucher and Vincent 2000, 185–209).

One of the reasons for my belated attention to Collingwood is that this significant academic philosopher devoted so much of his scholarly time to philosophical methods of historical interpretation—including the interpretation of historically influential philosophical works. Collingwood's methodology has received close examination in many of the great works in the field of hermeneutics or interpretative studies. Gadamer, for example, devotes considerable attention in his monumental work *Truth and Method* to Collingwood's famous 'logic of question and answer' and also to two of Collingwood's works: *An Autobiography* and *The Idea of History* (Gadamer 1979, 333–341, 467–469). It appears from this type of recognition that Collingwood has a lot to say about relationships between truth and method; yet we find that Gadamer eventually declares that he does 'not seriously differ from Strauss' who wrote a lengthy critical appraisal rejecting Collingwood's methods of textual interpretation (Gadamer 1979, 486). Even though Strauss's criticism of Collingwood does not feature at all prominently in the academic commentary on Collingwood, it would seem that Strauss thought it important to try to demonstrate some of the pitfalls of Collingwood's interpretative methods (Strauss 1952).

We will get more closely into Collingwood's methods of textual interpretation soon. But my own method in this chapter starts with a review of Claude Lefort's interest in the art of writing political theory. This review builds on earlier commentary on Lefort in Chapter 2 of this book. Here I examine aspects of his identification of the importance of Leo Strauss as a model for the historical interpretation of political theory texts. Putting Lefort's praise of Strauss to the test, I then look more closely at Strauss's detailed and quite critical examination of the techniques of textual interpretation developed by Collingwood—published in the same year as the book *Persecution and the Art of Writing* relied on by Lefort (Strauss 1952). My own interpretation is that Collingwood does not necessarily suffer from all of the defects identified by Strauss, who was directing his attention to a version of Collingwood's philosophy of history published after his death—'edited posthumously by his pupil T. M. Knox', with a more recent editor noting 'the rather complicated way this book has come about', with several draft chapters being deleted. Clearly, the first editor Knox was guilty of 'manipulation of the text'; further, there are 'reasons to doubt whether Knox has always been as scrupulous in editing *The Idea of History* as one should have wished' (Connelly and D'Oro 2008, v–vi, xiv, xviii, xix). My recovery of an alternative articulation by Collingwood comes from my reading of an earlier work not cited by Strauss: the 1933 book on 'method' with its unusual defence of the literary form of philosophical writing.

My contention is that Collingwood's 1933 text on 'method' nicely summarises ways that we today can learn to see how important it is for academic teachers to 'teach the text' in literary form as well as intellectual substance. Missing from Strauss's detailed study is any mention of Collingwood's 1933 work. One implication could be that this earlier work is less affected by the 'historicism' Strauss found in Collinwood's later works, especially his 1946 *The Idea of History*. What I shall briefly examine here is the contribution to interpretations of modern political theory found in the lengthy chapter ten called 'Philosophy as a Branch of Literature' (Collingwood 2008, 199–220). Strauss famously used all of his critical force to demonstrate many of the potential limitations of the posthumous and badly edited version of historical interpretation. Yet it is possible that Collingwood's earlier explicit book on 'method' might qualify some of this critique by Strauss, whose own *Persecution and the Art of Writing* dovetails so well with many of Collingwood's reflections.

THE RELEVANCE OF LEFORT

In Chapter 2, I referred to Claude Lefort's *Writing* as an exemplary study of the art of writing (Lefort 2000). I have also used Lefort's own study of the art of writing in my chapter on Machiavelli's *The Prince*. Here, I want to return to Lefort's essays on writing and reading because of the role he has identified for Strauss in modelling methods for interpreting political theory texts. Lefort's 'Three Notes on Leo Strauss' is not the sort of academic article to be read by new students to the academic study of political theory; but this article can help academic teachers of political theory learn more about methods of textual interpretation (Lefort 2000, 172–206).

How does this use of Lefort relate to English philosopher R. G. Collingwood? Lefort's earlier (and quite lengthy) chapter on Machiavelli refers extensively to Strauss's 1958 'great work' *Thoughts on Machiavelli*, with Strauss described as worthy of 'the homage' Lefort bestows on him—for providing 'the most penetrating critique' of Machiavelli (Lefort 2000, 111, 121–122). Clearly Lefort sees Strauss as a critic who understands the distinctive art of writing used in grand political theory. Lefort's series of notes examining Strauss have around 96 footnotes, the first of which refers to Strauss's 1952 book *Persecution and the Art of Writing* where Strauss promoted his controversial views about various forms of 'persecution' (from political or religious retribution to social ostracism) thought by philosophical writers to convince them to write strategically—hiding their deepest thoughts from suspicious readers who might be potential opponents, while leaving enough carefully disguised evidence to arouse closer interest in their deeper theory by potential allies (Lefort 2000, 204). These notes examine Strauss's concept of the art of writing found in *Persecution and the Art of Writing*'s analysis of classic political theorists coping with the risks and consequences of persecution—and also in the later *Thoughts on Machiavelli* book examining

Machiavelli's cagy art of writing. Lefort describes Strauss not as a 'historian of ideas' but as 'a philosopher-interpreter' using his 'unmatched acuity' to 'restitute the design' of great works—'as their authors themselves conceived it' (Lefort 2000, 179, 202). If Lefort is correct, then Strauss is indeed a rare model of the 'philosopher-interpreter' useful when teaching new students how to read classics in the history of modern political theory.

Missing from Lefort's analysis is reference to this other 1952 publication by Strauss also dealing with issues of interpretation: 'On Collingwood's Philosophy of History' (Strauss 1952). This article is also neglected by many scholars of Collingwood, even though it is one of Strauss's only investigations of Collingwood's theories of interpretation—and one of Strauss's early formulations of his case against historicism. Put simply, 'historicism' is the interpretative scheme drawn from the philosophy of history which denies that we today can look back into the history of political thought and understand works of political theory 'as their authors themselves conceived it'. We can have views about what these past authors wrote but we can have no certainty about knowing their thought as the authors originally conceived it. The problem is not that the authors wrote to disguise or hide some of their deepest thoughts; the real problem is that their thought is so deeply influenced and shaped by their historical context that it is little more than a product of their times, with very little capacity to speak to us today in our own terms, which inevitably reflect the changing context of historical development.

COLLINGWOOD'S QUESTIONS ANSWERED

Collingwood's *The Idea of History* is now available in a revised edition but with no reference to Strauss's review essay (Collingwood 1993). Strauss made use of Collingwood in a number of other places, included one of his examinations of 'Heideggerian Existentialism' (see e.g. Strauss 1989, 34). Thomas Pangle notes that Strauss appreciated Collingwood's 'lucid articulations' of political philosophy while criticising his interpretative methodology of question and answer (Pangle 2006, 144, note 17). It is Strauss's critique of that interpretative methodology in *The Idea of History* we should now briefly examine.

Strauss is struck with Collingwood's statement that 'all history is the history of thought' (Strauss 1952, 560). Can it be that we today can rethink or re-enact or relive or reproduce past thought? Strauss seems to hope that Collingwood will provide a positive answer and that scholars of past political thought will then be able to carry out that task of rethinking. Strauss notes that Collingwood believes that rethinking or re-enacting past thought requires critical engagement with that thought. Criticism could be either positive or negative. Positive criticism could arise from our professional role as philosophers who love wisdom as distinct from historians who might simply love the past. Alternatively, negative criticism could arise from some kind of tension or competition between the past and our present, especially if we thought that both past and present were framed and perhaps even hedged or locked in by their historical contexts. Strauss reckons that Collingwood either takes a negative perspective on the role of criticism or otherwise modifies the prospect of positive perspectives of criticism. The larger point is that Strauss contends that Collingwood is in a dilemma and perhaps more broadly reflects a dilemma characteristic of our age of historicism: we seem to know more and more about the past, including past political theory, but we also seem to doubt that we can ever really understand the past as it was understood by those in the past whose thought we want to understand. All our norms of criticism are held to reflect the norms of our own historical context, with the implication that we will gather more information about the past but never really understand the apparently *abnormal* past. What little we claim to know about the past is not enough to enable us properly to engage in criticism of the past.

For Strauss, Collingwood displayed in *The Idea of History* a 'failure to clarify his position sufficiently' (Strauss 1952, 564). In general, Strauss devotes quite a lot of space to articulating with great care what he thinks Collingwood is trying to do with his techniques of interpretation. Strauss forces himself to make the best case for the framework of interpretation Collingwood is trying to argue: friends of Collingwood will find Strauss striving to present a thesis illustrating Collingwood at his best. Yet at a certain point, Strauss concedes: 'Some critical remarks seem to be necessary' (Strauss 1952, 568). This criticism reflects Strauss at his best: praising Collingwood but praising the truth even more. The sympathetic side of Strauss's assessment is that Collingwood was a model of historical curiosity who provided great support for those wanting to practice historical research and to try to understand past texts containing important examples of philosophy and political theory. The negative side of Strauss's critique was that Collingwood's logic of question and answer did not help historians look at past thought 'from the point of view of the earlier thinkers' (Strauss 1952, 566).

Strauss's review article is in two parts. The first part ends with a comparison between Collingwood's sympathetic but somewhat colourless picture of how the classical Greeks thought of history, and Strauss's alternative picture of history as it featured in Greek political theory. This section is one of Strauss's notable portraits of classical Greek thinking as an alternative to contemporary philosophies of historicism (see e.g. Strauss 1952, 568–573). The second part allows Strauss to generalise beyond classical Greece by arguing that earlier thinkers about history were 'more careful readers than we have become' (Strauss 1952, 574). Collingwood's belief in what Strauss called 'the equality of all ages' should have allowed him to understand past thought 'on its own terms'; yet he tended to equalise historical perspectives, so that 'the past's self-interpretation' is no more important than 'our interpretation of the thought of the past'. Since this tends to dominate our way of thinking, we slowly cease to bother to try to 'take seriously the way in which the thought of the past understood itself' (Strauss 1952, 574). Instead, Collingwood acts as a representative of contemporary historicism by trying to understand past thought in what appears to be a reductive sense: reading past thought 'in the light of its time', despite the possibility that thought can be untimely, even revolutionary (Strauss 1952, 575). Thus, the quest for historical 're-enactment' proves next to impossible because Collingwood rejects that we can truly understand past thought as it was understood by those who wrote the great texts we look to when learning about past thought.

Strauss suggests that Collingwood is unduly persuaded by a certain belief in historical progress, with the implication that past thought can be retained as we progress forward, steadily supplementing past thoughts with newer thoughts. This makes it seem that we today can simply walk around our historical museums and in each room re-enter and so retain the types of past thought once dominating times gone by. Strauss makes an important comparison: while Collingwood believes that we can *retain* past thought, Strauss contends that we have to work hard to *recover* past thought—and that this intellectual recovery will require special types of interpretation (Strauss 1952, 578). The thought of the past has to 'be known as it actually was, i.e., as it was actually thought by past thinkers'—and so understanding past thought 'as its author consciously meant it' (Strauss 1952, 578, 581). Contrasting

Collingwood's logic of question and answer with his alternative logic of interpretation, Strauss demands that historians of political thought must 'rigorously subordinate' the historians' questions to 'the question which the author of his sources meant to answer': e.g. 'what question was uppermost in Herodotus' mind'—that is, 'the question regarding the perspective in which Herodotus looked at things' (Strauss 1952, 581). Historians of political thought might even have to 'retract his own question in favour of the questions raised by the authors of his sources' (Strauss 1952, 582).

For Strauss, the historian is 'necessarily a critic' whose interpretation is shaped by 'the critical judgment' of the importance of the themes under investigation (Strauss 1952, 582). Siding at times with Collingwood, Strauss argues that historical interpretation involves critical appraisal of 'the supporting reasoning' which often makes up 'the teaching of an author'—some of whom seem comfortable with 'the inevident character of the premises' featured in their works. Criticism of those premises might in some instances result in 'a criticism of present day thought from the point of view of the thought of the past' (Strauss 1952, 583). In a very long paragraph on the related roles of criticism and interpretation, Strauss sees the written texts of political theory as the sources for the historian's interpretation and unwritten philosophy as the source for the criticism historians might then make of the interpreted text. The suggestion is that understanding requires both interpretation and criticism (Strauss 1952, 184–185).

I close this section by noting that Strauss did not republish this review article in any of his later collections of his republished writings. One can suspect that he knew there was something wrong with the 1946 edition of Collingwood's *The Idea of History*. One would be right, as was mentioned earlier in this chapter: the later 2008 edition corrects many errors in the original edition reviewed by Strauss, who would generally have valued much of what Collingwood says about textual interpretation. So partly to recover Collingwood's own interpretation, I turn now to two other texts he wrote displaying a more solid framework for interpretation and criticism.

COLLINGWOOD'S LITERARY INTERPRETATION

Strauss had other works by Collingwood he could have noted in his review essay. Of particular importance is Collingwood's *An Autobiography* first published in 1939, with a philosophical temper very akin to that of Strauss—and dedicated to the proposition that 'all history is the history of thought' (Collingwood 1944, 75). In this autobiography, Collingwood pays special attention to the what he calls 'political theory', as though this term conveniently identifies the subject matter of very close importance to this intellectual historian—although we should note those instances when Collingwood prefers to speak of 'the history of political thought' as an alternative to 'political theory' (see e.g. Collingwood 1944, 37, 75, 100). He also identifies which of his own works he thinks his 'best book' in terms of its 'matter'—indeed what he calls his 'only book' when it comes to 'style' (Collingwood 1944, 80). This is *An Essay on Philosophical Method* first published in 1933. Shortly I will try to say why I think this judgment points us to an important theme for our conclusion, which is the place of 'style' in political theory.

Also relevant here is that Collingwood devotes much of his attention in his autobiography to his logic of question and answer (Collingwood 1944, 24–33). The version given in the autobiography contains less of the equivocation and much less of the intellectual dilemma identified by Strauss in his review. In defending his interpretative logic, Collingwood makes a case for the activity of 'interpretation' taking precedence over the activity of 'criticism', so that historical inquiry can focus as much as it can on the questions posed by past writers well ahead of the 'critical' task of making philosophical judgment about the truth or falsity of the answers circulating in the historical texts. Collingwood goes further, even suggesting that the task for the interpreters is to follow the text wherever it might lead them, regardless of the personal criticism they might be tempted to make about the falsity or errors of dated philosophical answers (Collingwood 1944, 32, 44, 46).

He contrasts two types of answers we can uncover when interpreting historical texts: one is the 'right' one appropriate to the text under examination and the other is the 'true' one as it might appear to our critical judgment. Collingwood generally holds that textual interpretation should follow the former and suspend the latter. He insists that certain types of historical texts will tease us with what appear to be 'untrue' answers: and he reveals why this might occur, as when (citing the case of Plato) 'a thinker is following a false scent, either inadvertently or in order to construct a *reductio ad absurdum*'. In the example given from Plato's *Republic*, Collingwood argues that a 'false' set of answers—in this case from Polemarchus in Book 1 of the *Republic*—'constitutes a link, and a sound one, in the chain of questions and answers by which the falseness of that presupposition is made manifest' (Collingwood 1944, 30).

The important implication is that Plato as the author has a good reason for letting some of the characters in the *Republic* make intellectual mistakes. This version of the logic of question and answer helps Collingwood link together the two arts of writing and reading. His interest in interpretative strategies becomes more general as he investigates 'rules in the study of philosophical texts', where one of his core themes is stated simply as 'how to read a philosophical text' (Collingwood 1944, 53). He appreciates that historical texts vary very much from one another and that the questions posed by each author are unlikely to match or duplicate those of other authors. The questions posed by Plato were not the same questions posed by Hobbes; in both cases, interpreters have to follow the answers as they appear in the texts of Plato and Hobbes, declining in both cases to substitute their own critical judgment about what might be the 'right' answers—at least until one has understood everything in their texts, as well as the interpreters, think their authors wanted to be understood (Collingwood 1944, 46).

Collingwood's Literary Method

If *An Essay on Philosophical Method* is thought by Collingwood to be his best book, then we wonder what the author might have thought about the generally negative reviews it received. One reviewer considered the book's mode of argument 'heroic rather than convincing', displaying 'an Oxonian pose, which looks ludicrous' (Schiller 1934, 118–120). Another reviewer noted the final chapter 'on philosophy as a branch of literature' before confessing that: 'I have no space to discuss' this chapter (Russell 1934, 350–352). Yet another reviewer noted Collingwood's 'high literary quality' before declaring that 'Collingwood wholly fails to establish any of the premises upon which he bases his methodical conclusions' which are 'demonstrably false' (Ducasse 1936, 95–106). Rare are the reviewers like the one who highlighted the last chapter's writing for its 'lucidity, precision, and occasional beauty' (Murphy 1935, 191–192). The editors of the current edition quote the published judgment of A. J. Ayer that Collingwood's work 'is a contribution to belles-lettres rather than philosophy. The style is uniformly elegant, the matter mostly obscure' (Connelly and D'Oro 2008, xxxix).

It is clear from these rebuttals that Collingwood's essay failed to persuade its readers to support the author's 'method'. The chapter on philosophy as literature is the penultimate chapter, followed by a 'conclusion' of around six pages (Collingwood 2008, 221–226). This brief conclusion defends the 'philosophical method' promised in the book's title against what its opponents might describe it as 'a tissue of cobwebs, a house of cards, a castle in the air'. The language here suggests that the author well-understood how little he would be understood. Concepts can be defined in so many ways, with many different consequences 'for the writer and reader of philosophical literature'. Defending his own attempt to define concepts that would promote 'deepening and widening of our knowledge', Collingwood invites readers to consider whether his 'method' really 'is consonant with experience'. Acknowledging his 'double procedure' by which he has made his analysis not only 'categorical' (i.e. consistent with premises) but also 'existential' (i.e. consistent with 'actual experience'), Collingwood warns readers not to expect too much 'dialectic of pure reason' given the rise of modern scepticism. Based on this scepticism, what 'actual experience' really matters? Collingwood's answer appears very 'traditional' as he terms it: 'the history of European thought' which might well be reappraised as 'a chaos of discordant ravings' (Collingwood 2008, 225).

The view of 'the historian of thought' is that history matters in the specific sense that a 'tradition' of philosophy can be discovered by 'historical study' and indeed 'philosophical criticism': two terms very close, I think, to our earlier set of Collingwood's terms of 'interpretation' and 'criticism'. The last word of the conclusion is 'progress': Collingwood notes that some thinkers (Nietzsche perhaps?) have been sceptical about scepticism and doubted that the history of thought is indeed 'a history of achievement and progress'. This retreat from progressive history leaves those retreating susceptible to 'ridicule and disgust' (Collingwood 2008, 225).

The penultimate chapter is organised into five parts and these are organised into 20 sections. Readers might expect a degree of complexity from this chapter with so confusing an arrangement of compartments. The comments which follow track in turn each of the five large parts.

Part one begins the examination of what could well be the perspective generating that notable 'ridicule and disgust' identified by Collingwood. Tentatively, we might expect to find a philosophy of history celebrating the concept of progress. Instead, we find a philosophy of literature with progressive examples of philosophy occurring throughout history.

We can read this as Collingwood's 'tradition' of 'philosophical literature': in particular, prose works which are in a formal sense *beautiful* and in a material sense *true*. The writers of such works must then be artists as well as thinkers. The matter is prior to the form, so that the 'garment of words' are, as it were, determined by the matter: prose writers have something 'to say' and they are unlike writers of poetry who try 'simply to speak' (Collingwood 2008, 199–200).

Part two presents a claim that philosophy is 'a kind of literature', different in kind from science or history. Many of the greatest philosophers 'have written well in addition to thinking well', often rejecting a technical vocabulary, with many key terms shifting their meaning 'from one writer to another'. Collingwood notes that 'every careful reader of the great philosophers' knows that these writers used 'a literary language'. He explains that the 'duty of a philosopher as a writer' is to choose his words 'according to the rules of literature' where words have 'that flexibility, that dependence upon context' consistent with literary use. A 'corresponding duty' for the reader is to be aware that they are 'reading a language' and not collecting core concepts or parsing definitions. The flexibility of language 'is what makes it able to express its own meaning' compared to the rigidity of 'artificial technical terms'. Collingwood notes that technical terms are 'not used in ordinary speech'. The claim is that 'ordinary language' has two characteristics: groups of words with 'shades of meaning' and single words used in 'various senses' (Collingwood 2008, 201–208).

Part three is the central part of this concluding chapter, comparing the two writing arts of philosophy and history, both of which 'demand artistic writing' but with differences in 'style'. Historians tend to have 'a slightly dogmatic and hectoring tone' with their 'attempt to impress and convince'. Philosophers are more confessional, free from the 'bombast' of historians. The writing of history is very selective, with authors tending to suppress anything known only in a doubtful way, which gives the writer 'an air of knowing more than he says'; history books are 'instructive or didactic in style', with the author separated from the reader who never really knows what processes of thought have been relied on or rejected by the writer. Philosophy differs in a fundamental way. Philosophical authors write 'primarily' to themselves and so they 'never instruct or admonish their readers'. Whereas historians tend to conceal problems, philosophers tend to confess their difficulties. Those philosophers who have had 'the deepest instinct for style' have 'repeatedly shrunk from adopting the form of a lecture or instructive address'. Their alternative preference is for 'a dialogue' with a cast of characters or 'a mediation' reflecting alone or 'a dialectical process' with repeated changes to an initial position 'as difficulties in it come to light'. Readers 'consult' historians; but they 'follow' philosophers. Readers of philosophy 'understand what they think, and reconstruct it ourselves, so far as we can, the processes by which they have come to think it'. Readers of works of philosophy hope that they can be 'living through the same experience that his author lived through' (Collingwood 2008, 208–212).

Part four examines the activity of 'learning to write philosophy' (Collingwood 2008, 213). Philosophy can be very much like poetry. Many of 'the greatest philosophers', and certainly the best philosophical writers, have 'adopted an imaginative and somewhat poetic style': Collingwood gives as an example the dialogue form used by Plato but he also refers to 'the classical elegance of Descartes', the 'lapidary phrases of Spinoza', Hegel's 'tortured metaphor-ridden periods'. None of these are 'defects in philosophical expression' or 'signs of defects in philosophical thought'. As writers, philosophers 'go to school with the poets' and this requires: 'skill in metaphor and simile, readiness to find new meanings in old words, ability in case of need to invent new words and phrases which shall be understood as soon as they are heard, and briefly a disposition to improvise and create, to treat language as something not fixed and rigid but infinitely flexible and full of life' (Collingwood 2008, 214). The art of the philosopher-writer 'is an art that must conceal itself', displaying not the show of great jewels but the hard work of 'a lens-grinder'. He uses literary techniques like metaphor and imagery 'just so far as to reveal thought, and no farther'.

Part five is the final instalment of this chapter. Readers of Strauss's review of Collingwood might recall its complicated conclusion dealing with relationships between interpretation and criticism (see e.g. Strauss 1952, 583–586). Worth comparing is Collingwood's own conclusion where he relates the two activities of 'comprehension' and 'criticism' (Collingwood 2008, 215–220). Collingwood writes quite extensively here about the role of readers in comprehending and criticising writers. The theme comes surprisingly from poetry, with the suggestion that readers have to think of writers as poets, with both writer and reader striving to 'live through' similar experiences. Readers have to try to discover 'the writer's mind with his own'. This reference to 'mind' implies that readers have to comprehend not simply the *words* in a text but the *mind* of the author of that text. Collingwood warns us that 'the task of criticizing' is 'altogether secondary'. Readers have to put aside their own critical assumptions and 'follow where he is led' instead of trying to 'find a path of his own'. Putting aside criticism, readers need to bring 'this silent, uninterrupting attention' to their reading. Readers have to train themselves when reading these great books 'to follow it in its movement' and not prematurely condemn the work 'as illogical or unintelligible'. Comprehension and criticism are closely related intellectual activities, both of which are required to complete the project of understanding a great writer's great work. However, comprehension is prior to criticism. The argument is that 'a good reader must keep quiet and refrain from obtruding his own thoughts when trying to understand author'. The primary task is to follow the author's thought and to try to reconstruct 'the point of view from which it proceeds'. The critic 'works from within', by trying to supplement the author's account 'by adding certain aspects which the author has overlooked'. Critics thus 'develop and continue the thought of the writer criticized' (Collingwood 2008, 215–220).

Conclusion

The two themes of performance and pedagogy are now sketched in sufficient detail that we can see how they relate to writing and reading political theory. Collingwood, Strauss and Lefort are unusually gifted academic scholars whose works fill out the framework of interpretation. Academic teachers of political theory can learn how to make use of their scholarly debates to show students what interpretative performance means for those studying political theory.

Readers of Strauss's critique of Collingwood might recall a phrase about the importance of 'the teaching of an author as the author understood it' (Strauss 1952, 582). Not all historians of political thought write about 'the teaching' of authors. Strauss generally does, assuming that part of the very real importance of a thinker's written thoughts is the teaching they convey. Collingwood generally refers to the philosophy these thinker-writers might convey, although his close attention to the careful preparation taken by his most valued readers suggests that there is a kind of teaching being conveyed from writer to reader. I think that both Strauss and Collingwood held that many of the most important political theorists in the Western, including modern, tradition took pedagogy seriously. In both Strauss and Collingwood we see this interest in pedagogy at a very high level, with both historians of political theory arguing that the greatest writer-thinkers cultivated something of a critical or what we now call disruptive pedagogy, designed perhaps to reform established or conventional political understandings—to cultivate critical thinking free from political establishments. I think that Strauss's review of Collingwood prepares us to learn that a very great historian of political theory like Collingwood is also a very great educator, capable of using his own intellectual talents to echo many of the most impressive historical political theorists in using his writing to continue to teach readers even today about the nature and role of political theory.

Lefort claimed that Strauss was not simply a historian of ideas but also a 'philosopher-interpreter' (Lefort 2000, 179). This chapter ties together many of the themes of performance and pedagogy in political theory with an examination of the activity of textual interpretation. I think that Collingwood stands alongside Strauss as a 'philosopher-interpreter'. Just as Strauss helps us see and learn to understand much of the humour hidden in historical works of political theory, I think that Collingwood too writes in ways that appeal to our humour. I do not know how seriously he wanted readers to follow his strict line of black-letter argument in *An Essay on Philosophical Method* about the many differences between historians and philosophers. Like Strauss, Collingwood was capable of writing either form of written work or indeed combining both forms in one work. It is unclear whether his voice in this important chapter is purely philosophical or somewhat reflecting the voice of a historian. His comparative portrait forces us as readers to think all that more carefully about how we practice the many arts of political history and political philosophy. I think this book will have done its job if a few more academic teachers of the history of political theory reflect more astutely on the methods of interpretation clarified by Strauss and Collingwood.

In closing, I recall that in the Preface to this book I warned readers that my interest in pedagogy related to teaching English-language versions of texts to English-language students. The highly skilled interpretative schemes debated by Collingwood, Strauss and Lefort live well beyond these practical limitations. Academic teachers responsible for courses in the history of modern political theory would normally not expect their students to know about issues of interpretation at this deeper level. Our own performance as academic teachers can be shaped and informed by the exciting scholarship of Collingwood, Strauss and Lefort; and it might also be so that some of the very best students might welcome the challenge of working through this remarkable scholarship. However, the starting point remains at a much simpler level. Our teaching task is to help new students read a range of old books. Should these new readers respond well to our criticism, then we can invite them to think through with us the schemes of textual interpretation pioneered by Collingwood, Strauss and Lefort, each of whom enjoyed performing as political theorists as they wrote so remarkably about the arts of writing and reading.

REFERENCES

Boucher, David, and Andrew Vincent. 2000. *British Idealism and Political Theory*. Edinburgh: Edinburgh University Press.
Collingwood, R.G. 1944. *An Autobiography*. Harmondsworth, Middlesex: Pelican Books.
Collingwood, R.G. 1989. *Essays in Political Philosophy*, ed. David Boucher. Oxford: Clarendon Press.
Collingwood, R.G. 1993. *The Idea of History*, Revised ed., edited with an Introduction by Jan Van Der Dussen. Oxford: Clarendon Press.
Collingwood, R.G. 2008. *An Essay on Philosophical Method*, ed. James Connelly and Giuseppina D'Oro. Oxford: Clarendon Press.
Connelly, James, and Giuseppina D'Oro. 2008. Editors' Introduction. In *An Essay on Philosophical Method*, ed. R.G. Collingwood, xiii–cxii. Oxford: Clarendon Press.
Ducasse, C.J. 1936. Mr. Collinwood on Philosophical Method. *The Journal of Philosophy* 33 (4): 95–106.
Gadamer, Hans-Georg. 1979. *Truth and Method*, 2nd ed. trans. William Glen-Doepel. London: Sheed and Ward.
Henze, Donald. 1980. The Style of Philosophy. *The Monist* 63 (4): 417–424.
Lefort, Claude. 2000. *Writing: The Political Test*, trans. and ed. David Ames Curtis. Durham: Duke University Press.
Murphy, Arthur E. 1935. Review. *The Philosophical Review* 44 (2): 191–192.
Pangle, Thomas. 2006. *Leo Strauss: An Introduction to His Thought and Intellectual Legacy*. Baltimore: Johns Hopkins University Press.
Russel, L.J. 1934. Review. *Philosophy* 9 (35): 350–352.
Schiller, F.C.S. 1934. New Books. *Mind* 43 (169): 118–120.
Strauss, Leo. 1952. On Collingwood's Philosophy of History. *Review of Metaphysics* 5 (4): 559–586.
Strauss, Leo. 1989. *The Rebirth of Classical Political Rationalism*. Selected and Introduced by Thomas Pangle. Chicago: University of Chicago Press.

Erratum to: Performing Political Theory

Erratum to:
J. Uhr, *Performing Political Theory*,
https://doi.org/10.1007/978-981-10-7998-6

In the original version of the book, the belated corrections from author in Frontmatter, Chapters 1, 2, 3, 4, 6 and 7 have been incorporated. The erratum book has been updated with the changes.

The updated online version of this book can be found at
https://doi.org/10.1007/978-981-10-7998-6_1
https://doi.org/10.1007/978-981-10-7998-6_2
https://doi.org/10.1007/978-981-10-7998-6_3
https://doi.org/10.1007/978-981-10-7998-6_4
https://doi.org/10.1007/978-981-10-7998-6_6
https://doi.org/10.1007/978-981-10-7998-6_7
https://doi.org/10.1007/978-981-10-7998-6

© The Author(s) 2018
J. Uhr, *Performing Political Theory*,
https://doi.org/10.1007/978-981-10-7998-6_8

Index

A
Alexander VI, 64
Alexander, Edward, 75
American Political Science Association (ASPA), vi, 5
Arendt, Hannah, vii
Aristotle, viii, 10, 11, 43, 79
Ashley Cooper, Anthony. *See* Shaftesbury, Lord
Austen, Jane, 33
Austin, J.L., 2–4
Australian Research Council, viii
Ayer, A.J., 111

B
Bacon, Francis, ix, 20, 21, 23–25, 30
Bentham, Jeremy, 77
Berlin, Isaiah, 53–55, 62
Bloom, Allan, 5
Bonaparte, Napoleon, 93
Borgia, Cesare, 61–66
Boston College, ix
Bosworth, William, v, viii, ix
Buckle, Henry Thomas, 93
Burke, Kenneth, 55
Burns, Timothy, viii–ix
Butler, Judith, 2–3

C
Cambridge University, ix
Cassirer, Ernst, 47–48
Clark, Karen, ix
Coleridge, Samuel Taylor, 77
Collingwood, R.G., 29, 102–117

D
Daryanomel, Vishal, ix
De Grazia, Sebastian, 52–53
Descartes, Rene, 114
Dewey, John, 20, 21, 23–27, 29, 30
Diamond, Martin, 5

E
Enlightenment, the, 20

F
Faulkner, Robert, ix
Finifter, Ada, vi

G
Gadamer, Hans-Georg, 104
Ginsberg, Robert, 46
Gladstone, William, viii
Green, J.E., 7
Grube, Dennis, ix

H
Habermas, Jurgen, 7
Hegel, Georg, 114
Herodotus, 109
Hobbes, Thomas, vi, 13, 34, 48, 103, 111
Homer, 93
Hume, David, 46

I
International Political Education Database (IPED), 7

J
Johnson, J.A., 7

K
Kant, Immanuel, vi, 14
Knox, T.M., 104

L
Lang, Berel, 47
Lefort, Claude, 17, 27–29, 102, 104, 105–106, 116, 117
Livy, 59, 60

Locke, John, vi, 11–13, 23, 34, 37, 46, 48

M
Machiavelli, Niccolo, v, vi, 2, 4, 9, 10, 12–15, 17, 20, 22, 27, 28, 51–66, 86, 87, 101, 102, 105
Macpherson, C.B., vi
Markley, Robert, 46–47
Marx, Karl, 87
Masters, Adam, 24
Medici, Lorenzo de, 52, 56, 59, 60
Medici, Lorenzo de (the Magnificent), 56
Mill, John Stuart, viii, 9, 12, 16, 19, 20, 54, 69–82, 87, 88, 101, 102
Milton, John, 37, 44

N
Nietzsche, Friedrich, v, 4, 8, 12, 14, 16, 20, 23, 27, 28, 55, 85–98, 102, 112

O
Orwell, George, 27, 28

P
Pangle, Thomas, viii, 34, 106
Pericles, 79, 93, 95
Petrarch, 58, 60
Plato, 48, 75, 79, 110–111, 114
Pocock, J.G.A, 5
Political Studies Association, 7

R
Rawls, John, 13
rhetoric, 21, 22, 37
Richetti, John J., 47

Richter, Melvin, 5
Romulus, 59, 62
Rousseau, Jean-Jacques, vi, 28, 46, 75, 77, 92
Rushdie, Salman, 27, 28
Ryle, Gilbert, 33

S

Saxonhouse, Arlene, vii, viii, 7
Schopenhauer, Arthur, 90
Sforza, 64
Shaftesbury, Lord, 11–12, 21, 30, 33–48, 102
Shklar, Judith, vii
Skinner, Quentin, vii, 7
Socrates, 75, 77
Spencer, Herbert, 93
Spinoza, Baruch, 47, 114
Strauss, Leo, vii, 6–7, 29, 102, 104–110, 115–117

T

Taylor, Harriet, 73
textualism, 10
Tocqueville, Alexis de, 25, 27, 75

U

Uhr, John, viii–ix, 14

V

Viroli, Maurizio, 14, 56, 58
von Humboldt, Alexander, 71–72

W

Wagner, Richard, 90
Weerakoon, Anushangi, ix
Williams, Bernard, 5